My
Guardian
Angel

Also by Doreen Virtue, Ph.D.

My Guardian Angel

TRUE STORIES OF ANGELIC
ENCOUNTERS FROM THE READERS OF
WOMAN'S WORLD MAGAZINE

Doreen Virtue, Ph.D.
with Amy Oscar

HAY HOUSE, INC.
Carlsbad, California • New York City
London • Sydney • Johannesburg
Vancouver • Hong Kong • New Delhi

Copyright © 2008 by Doreen Virtue and Heinrich Bauer North America, Inc.

Published and distributed in the United States by: Hay House, Inc.: www. hayhouse.com • *Published and distributed in Australia by:* Hay House Australia Pty. Ltd.: www.hayhouse.com.au • *Published and distributed in the United Kingdom by:* Hay House UK, Ltd.: www.hayhouse.co.uk • *Published and distributed in the Republic of South Africa by:* Hay House SA (Pty), Ltd.: www.hayhouse.co.za • *Distributed in Canada by:* Raincoast: www.raincoast.com • *Published in India by:* Hay House Publishers India: www.hayhouse.co.in

Editorial supervision: Jill Kramer • *Design:* Tricia Breidenthal

Library of Congress Cataloging-in-Publication Data

Virtue, Doreen.
 My guardian angel : true stories of angelic encounters from Woman's world magazine readers / Doreen Virtue with Amy Oscar. -- 1st ed.
     p. cm.
 ISBN 978-1-4019-1753-1 (tradepaper)
 1. Angels. I. Oscar, Amy. II. Woman's world magazine. III. Title.
 BL477.V59 2008
 202'.15--dc22

                    2007008190

ISBN: 978-1-4019-1753-1

        11 10 09 08   4 3 2 1
             1st edition, January 2008

Printed in the United States of America

To God and the angels.
— **Doreen Virtue**

To Michael.
— **Amy Oscar**

CONTENTS

INTRODUCTION

by Doreen Virtue

Do you believe in angels? If you're like me, you do. Surveys consistently find that the vast majority of people (between 75 and 90 percent, depending on the poll) believe that angels are real. During my university training in psychology, I learned that what's considered "normal" by mental-health professionals is whatever the majority of people do. Using this line of thinking, then, it's normal to believe in angels!

I was raised in a metaphysical Christian household that discussed angels at Christmastime but didn't acknowledge them as relevant to everyday life. Yet, like many children, I could see and hear those Divine messengers who surround all of us. I quickly discovered that everyone (regardless of religion or behavior) has angels who guide, protect, and love them throughout their lives. It became apparent to me, too, that although we all have them, many people don't listen to their guidance.

I also learned that God gave us all free will. We're at liberty to choose joy, health, or even sorrow. God and the angels can't usurp this freedom; however, they *can* offer alternatives that would lead to happier and healthier outcomes. These suggestions come in the form of Divine guidance that we receive as intuitive feelings, thoughts, visions, and even inner words. If we follow this counsel, everything goes better in our lives.

Because we have free will, we must request help from God and the angels before they can intervene. It doesn't matter *how* we ask for their aid, whether as a prayer, a plea, an affirmation, a letter, a song, a demand, or even as worries. What matters is *that* we ask.

So, what *are* angels? Well, they're celestial spirit beings made by the same Creator Who made you and me. They're messengers of God, like postal carriers who connect Earth and Heaven. You have guardian angels with you right now who look past the surface and see your true inner beauty and Divinity. They love you unconditionally!

In addition to your guardian angels, your departed loved ones also watch over you. Although people technically aren't angels (since they have human egos and are therefore fallible), they can act in an angelic capacity and work in concert with them. Many of the stories you'll read about in this book are from individuals who received loving messages from their friends and family members in Heaven.

Ever since the angels saved my life during an armed car-jacking in 1995, I've taught workshops and written books and articles teaching that angels are real and that they want to communicate with us more often. I was especially excited when the editors of *Woman's World* magazine asked me to help them create a weekly angel-story column along with Amy Oscar.

Writing for the "My Guardian Angel" column has become a highlight of each week for me! So many of the *Woman's World* angel stories touched and inspired me that I asked Hay House if they would publish them in a book collection.

I believe that we've all had encounters with our angels, but we may not have recognized them as such. Angel experiences come in many forms . . . as you'll read about in the true stories contained in this book.

With love,
Doreen

INTRODUCTION

by Amy Oscar

I knew that working on a magazine column about angels with Doreen Virtue would be inspiring, interesting, and unusual. However, it wasn't until our column was canceled that I felt the true power of the angels begin to pulse through my life.

Magazines work a few months ahead of print deadline, so we'd already completed about ten weeks' worth of angel stories before the first issue containing our column hit the stands. By then, the concept had been run past a focus group, it had tested badly, and our editors had decided to kill the project. *Oh well,* I thought. *That's the magazine business.*

But the angels—and our readers—thought differently, and a week after the first column broke, an editorial assistant handed me 15 letters addressed to "angels."

I knew I was supposed to reply with a polite explanation: "Thanks for your interest, but the column has been canceled." Still, I couldn't resist reading a few. Expecting to find comments about the column—*love it, hate it,* whatever—I was surprised to find a priceless story of Divine intervention tucked into each envelope: *The angels saved my life. . . . The angels lent me comfort . . . . The angels gave me a reason to go on.*

Although it's completely contrary to my nature to go against the boss's orders, *something* made me resist sending those letters back. I placed them in a small wicker basket on my desk. After a month, I walked into my editor's office with three bushels overflowing with miraculous stories! Needless to say, *Woman's World* decided to bring back the "My Guardian Angel" column.

About a month later, the same week that we launched the revamped "My Guardian Angel" column, our editor-in-chief Stephanie Saible found a huge white feather under her desk. (I found one on my keyboard.) The angels had left a thank-you note!

I'd felt the presence of the Divine in my life before through inklings, intuition, or signs—I'd even been rescued by a mysterious stranger when my car ran out of gas on the Throgs Neck Bridge. But I still thought of the angels as an "out there" subject best confined to mystical texts and workshops. Those letters, and the stories they contained, showed me just how widespread and "down-to-earth" the angels' presence truly is.

They seemed to be everywhere—saving lives on highways and in homes, bringing comfort at accident scenes and in hospitals, whispering warnings, whisking children out of harm's way, sending us signs, and walking through dreams. Our readers' letters formed a pattern, affirming the angels' message: "We are with you in all ways, at all times."

After almost four years, the "My Guardian Angel" column is still one of the most beloved parts of *Woman's World*—and the angels' warm and playful presence has changed my life. If you ask, I'm sure that they'll transform yours, too.

The other day Doreen asked me, "What happens when you call people to tell them that their story has been chosen for the column?" She thought that you might like to know, too.

Well, I read every letter, returning the ones I simply can't use with a thank-you note (since we're grateful for every story we receive—and so are the angels). I file the rest by general category: *Highway Angels, Mysterious Strangers, Voices, Dreams, Rescues,* and so forth. . . .

Each week, I pull two related stories and phone each author for a brief personal interview. This is my favorite part of the job. I make a cup of tea and pull my box of tissues close, knowing how touching these conversations can be. When I call, there's always delight (although sometimes there are tears), and I feel as if I'm presenting the gift of a lifetime. With subjects who have lost someone dear to them, I'm especially conscious that my phone call may bring more pain—but it also seems to soothe. I've stopped being surprised (but I'll always be amazed) by how often I "happen" to call on a special anniversary or birthday or just after the writer asked for a sign.

After we talk, I write up the stories *Woman's World*-style and e-mail them to Doreen. She returns her comments, and it becomes my challenge to shorten them without losing the beauty or essence of her message. Next, a senior editor, Andrea Florczak, passes the column to Stephanie for final approval. It moves through production—from art to copyediting to proofreading—and each subject receives a call from one of our photo editors. Finally, Debbie Jackson, our editorial assistant, (who's an angel herself!) reminds me to send my notes and invoices, making sure each contributor gets paid.

A month or two later, it arrives on the newsstands, where you pick it up. On behalf of all of us at *Woman's World*, thanks for reading (and loving!) our magazine—and the "My Guardian Angel" column.

Angel blessings always,
Amy

Chapter One

ENTERTAINING ANGELS UNAWARES

Be not forgetful to entertain strangers:
for thereby some have entertained angels unawares.
— Apostle Paul (Hebrews 13:2)

The beloved quote above speaks to the fact that occasionally angels take on human form. Our guardian angels are always with us in spirit, and they provide help for us continually in the best possible way for each situation.

If you're extremely upset, you may not hear this subtle Divine guidance. That's when angels assume a human appearance to make sure that you hear their messages. For example, if your car is stuck in the snow, they may show up with a shovel or snowmobile to save the day. Whatever it takes, your angels are there for you.

These Heavenly messengers can look like ordinary folks, and you may not even realize you've met one. Yet there are a few common denominators within the hundreds of "strangers who are really angels" stories:

1. There's an aura of peacefulness surrounding the angel, which has a calming effect upon the person involved.

2. The angel appears from out of nowhere—for instance, suddenly arriving without a vehicle on a highway where help is needed.

3. The other telltale characteristic is that the angel disappears before the person has a chance to offer thanks.

In true angelic fashion, these celestial beings seem unconcerned with tokens of gratitude. They only care whether they've done their job . . . which they accomplish in miraculous ways, as you'll read about in the stories that follow.

An Angel to Hold My Hand

In our darkest hour, our angels nestle close, offering comfort, as Melissa Heye of Albuquerque shares:

My angel in the sky turned a sad occasion into a time of comfort.

When I received the phone call that my brother, Brian, was in a coma and might not make it, I raced to the airport and took the first flight out. Needless to say, I was a wreck, and as I walked onto the plane, a flight attendant approached and asked, "Are you okay?"

"No," I admitted, explaining the situation.

She sat me down and brought me some water. After takeoff, she asked my seatmate if he'd mind taking the last spot in first class so that she could sit with me. She had the most beautiful red hair with gentle, glowing highlights. And she spent almost the whole flight comforting me, occasionally getting up to help other passengers. *How would I have made it through without her?* I wondered.

Two days later, my brother passed away, and after his funeral, I dragged myself onto the return flight, despair crushing my heart and an anxiety attack threatening. As we hit cruising altitude, I was in a terrible state when the curtain between first class and coach opened . . . and there was my friend the flight attendant!

My heart flooded with relief as she came down the aisle and gently invited me into first class, where she was working. Again, she sat beside me for the rest of the flight, and her presence comforted me enormously.

Before we parted, I asked for her address so that I could send a note to thank her. And when I got home, I did so, writing: "You must be an angel." But my card came back marked ADDRESS UNKNOWN. At first I felt hurt. Then a big smile lit my face as I realized, *She actually was an angel!*

She certainly was! Angels can take on human form to help us during crises. And when Melissa's grief grew overwhelming, Heaven sent a compassionate redheaded angel to comfort and heal her. After all, *human* flight attendants are much too busy to sit with one passenger during a flight!

These beings, who look just like us, are called *incarnated angels*. And they often appear in stressful, fearful situations. They stay, offering gentle comfort until, their job complete, they disappear without a trace. Only then do we know that we've been touched by the Divine.

The angels say, "The more you feel afraid, the stronger our presence becomes. During your most frightening moments, we appear to you in earthly, material form to bring you rapid comfort and support. Although we are endlessly with you, we realize that there are certain times when you need to concretely feel and hear our love."

Call upon your angels the minute you feel afraid or alone.

The Angelic Lady

Have you been helped by an angel? Diane Richard of Boynton Beach, Florida, was—although she didn't know it at the time:

I was six months pregnant, driving with my sons—Tyler, six, and Kyle, three—when a car barreled through a red light and smashed into the passenger side of our SUV. Screaming, I reached for my boys but was thrown backward, my arm smashing through the driver's-side window.

I blacked out, then awoke as the car bounced back onto its wheels and stopped. Instantly, the passenger door opened, and a woman wearing purple scrubs slid in beside me. "Don't move," she soothed. "You have a back injury. The boys and the baby are okay. Everyone is going to be fine, including you."

She fashioned a tourniquet out of my sweater to stop the bleeding in my arm. Then she opened the rear door to get into the backseat. She calmed the boys before using my cell phone to call my husband and mother.

As she hung up, a firefighter arrived. "We're going to get everyone out," he promised. "Then we'll call your husband."

"The lady just called," I said.

"What lady?" he asked. As they secured me to a stretcher, the paramedic told me that witnesses had said there hadn't been any woman at the scene. "You must have imagined it," he said.

"Then who did this?" I asked, lifting my bandaged arm. "And who called us?" my mom and my husband wondered when they arrived.

"The lady," Tyler said. He'd seen her, too! Then, while viewing the wreckage, I gasped: No one could have opened the rear passenger door. The collision had smashed it shut! We'd been helped by an angel—and as she'd predicted, we were all fine!

Diane and her children needed immediate help, so her guardian angel took on human form. Diane didn't question the logic of how the woman was able to open a smashed car door or how she knew that Diane's back had been injured.

For her, the woman was a godsend . . . little did she know! Diane's rescuer's sudden appearance and disappearance and her prophetic reassurance that everyone would be fine are clues to her angelic origins. Her purple scrubs are a less obvious one. Purple is a highly spiritual color, and scrubs are symbolic of healing professionals.

The angels say, "When you are about to have an experience where our help is required, we are there before the incident occurs. It is our sacred honor to watch over you in every way."

If you think that you've met an angel, then you probably have.

The Unexpected Angel

What do angels look like? They don't always wear white robes. They might appear in an old-fashioned suit or even in the rags of a homeless person, as Brandy Sickles of Richford, Vermont, discovered:

I was 22 and pregnant when my husband left me. And one day while driving with my mother, I looked down at my swelling belly, and a wave of sadness washed over me. *No one cares about my baby or me,* I sniffed.

We'd paused at a stop sign, and as I lifted my head, there—in front of my face—was a bouquet of flowers, held inside my open window by a homeless man. "God loves you," he said with a smile. "Everything will be okay."

"Uh, thanks," I gulped as he stepped back. Instantly, the load of sadness lifted from my shoulders. And somehow, I knew that I *would* be just fine. . . . Today, remarried to a wonderful man and raising my daughter and our new son, I am!

How like the angels to send a messenger dressed as a homeless person to let Brandy know that she wasn't alone and remind her of all she did have.

The angels often send comfort through unusual messengers: animals, signs, and even old-fashioned gentlemen, as Carol Cooley of Sullivan, Indiana, writes:

I was working as a restaurant cashier when I learned that I had breast cancer. A single woman with no family to support me, I felt desperately vulnerable and alone and didn't know where to turn. Then, a few days before my surgery, an elderly gentleman approached my register.

With his old-fashioned suit and hat, he looked like someone from the 1940s. And when another cashier offered to help him, he nodded in my direction, saying, "No, thanks. I'll wait for her." But instead of handing me a restaurant check, he asked, "Do you believe in angels?"

"Well," I answered, "I know that the Bible mentions something about 'entertaining angels unawares.'"

He nodded, smiled, and leaned toward me. "You are not alone," he said. "We are all around to help you."

Huh? I thought, glancing right and left to see if anyone else had heard his odd comment. When I looked back, the gentleman was gone. "Where'd he go?" I asked the other cashier, who looked as stunned as I was. And although we searched the premises, we found no trace of him.

I noticed that after his visit all my worries seemed to vanish. And a few days later, after minor surgery, my doctor told me the joyful news: There was no need for a mastectomy or chemotherapy. I was going to be just fine!

Carol's angel in disguise sparked her faith that she'd recover. And his presence probably helped to heal her cancer.

The angels say, "If you feel afraid, you may miss our messages of love. That is when we send an earth angel to deliver our words to you."

When a stranger delivers comforting words out of the blue, it's likely a Heaven-sent message.

Angel on the Highway

The angels will always find a way to answer your request, as Joyce Benedict of Hyde Park, New York, shares:

I'd been hanging out at a friend's house one night when I realized: "It's 2:15 A.M.! I've got to get home." But as I began driving, I nervously had the thought that it hadn't been such a smart idea to drive so late at night. And then as if to prove my point, just as I approached a deserted stretch of highway, my car lights went out.

"No!" I cried, panicking as I flicked at the controls. But the lights wouldn't come on. Slowly, I eased my car to the side of the road. *What should I do?* I worried. *Is it safe to walk to a phone? Should I sit here all night?*

Instantly, I heard a tap at my window. I jumped, startled, as a young man peered through the glass. *Where did he come from?* I wondered, my heart pounding. I hadn't seen any car approaching. *And what sort of person would be wandering on the highway at this hour?*

"Your lights are out," the man said. "I can fix them if you'll pop the hood."

"Er . . . sure," I gulped, pulling the release button. He lifted the hood, and three seconds later all my lights came on! Amazed and grateful, I reached for my purse, offering, "Let me give you some money."

But when I turned back toward the window, he was gone. Several years have passed, and I've asked many mechanics what a person could have done to get my car lights working instantly. None of their answers explained what he did so quickly. I've come to realize that the man who'd arrived just when I needed him was an angel.

Stranded in the dark without lights, Joyce was in a dangerous situation. She needed Divine intervention to get home, so an angel took on human form to make sure that she got it.

The angels say, "Never hesitate to ask us for assistance! Just be open to all possibilities so that you will be sure to notice the help that we bring."

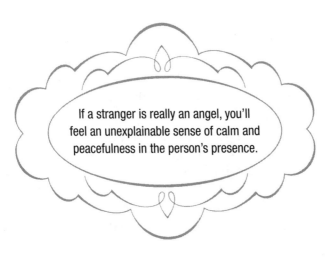

If a stranger is really an angel, you'll feel an unexplainable sense of calm and peacefulness in the person's presence.

The Airport Angel

Stuck in an airport? Your angels can ease travel stress—or even help you get home, as Anne M. Rogers of Oak Ridge North, Texas, recalls:

Some years ago, after my grandmother's 90th-birthday party, my two-year-old daughter, Kristen, and I flew out of Buffalo, New York, at 6:30 A.M. "We change planes in Newark," I told Kristen.

But once there, we were placed on standby. It was holiday time, so there were 14 other flights to Houston that day, and I felt certain that we'd soon be on our way. But by 8:30 P.M., I'd spent our last $10 on food for Kristen, and there was only one departure left!

Feeling desperate and tears threatening, I prayed: *Lord, I don't want to spend the night in the airport. Please help us get home tonight.* All at once, a nice-looking uniformed man approached the gate. "What are my chances of getting on this flight?" I asked him.

"Not promising," he said, checking the standby list. "You're number 52." He must have sensed my despair, because he started typing. And a moment later he said, "I've moved you up the list with a new name. When they announce 'Smith,' get on the plane."

Sure enough, "Smith" was called, and Kristen and I quickly boarded. Wanting to thank the man, I later asked my brother, who worked for the airline, to get his name. But my brother said, "That's strange. No man was scheduled to work at that gate."

But the story doesn't end there! A few years later, we visited Buffalo again, and our return flight was delayed. Arriving at Newark, we had less than ten minutes to make our connection. As we ran through the airport, I prayed, *Don't let us miss our flight!* But when we arrived, the Jetway door was closed. *Oh no!* I thought, tears welling.

Then from behind the gate wall, out stepped the same man: our hero! "We've held the plane for you," he said, smiling. Amazed, I gasped, "Thank you! But please tell me your name." Before he could answer, we were swept through the gate.

When I turned back, he was gone. And I suddenly knew that our hero in an airline uniform was truly an angel.

By praying for help, Anne enlisted Divine assistance immediately. Her angel took the appearance of an airport employee because that was the most efficient way to answer her prayer.

There are so many stories from people who were helped by guardian angels showing up in airports and on planes. Indeed, they seem to have an affinity for places involved with flight.

The angels say, "We hold your hand literally and figuratively throughout your life. Occasionally you are aware of our presence, yet most of the time you do not know that we are there. We have no need for credit or acknowledgment; however, we do want you to be assured that we are continuously available to support you in all ways."

Call upon the angels to stop or reduce turbulence when you're flying, and they'll stabilize the airplane.

The Christmas Eve Angels

During the holiday season, the angels seem to bring additional blessings to our lives, as Donna Kidman of Needham, Massachusetts, experienced:

It was Christmas Eve, and the snow was coming down hard. "I need to pick up some film," I told my children, ages two and four, as I pulled into the parking lot. We hurried to the store, heads down to avoid the driving snow, when suddenly I slammed face-first into a copper pipe that was hanging from the back of a truck. I could taste blood on my lip, but I had no idea how serious it was until the employee in the store gasped, "Should I call an ambulance?"

"I'll be fine," I said. The clerk gave me a towel and some ice. Then she led me to a mirror, where *I* was the one who gasped! I'd split my upper lip completely open and loosened a front tooth!

"I need stitches," I said. Instantly, my mind started racing. As a single mother, I was on my own. I couldn't drive my stick-shift car while holding the ice. The kids needed dinner, and when I was in the ER, who would watch them?

Just then a young couple entered the store. I couldn't help noticing that although every other customer came in covered with snow, the pregnant woman's jacket and that of her husband didn't have a trace of white, nor did their hatless heads.

"My name is Mary," the woman said. "Everything is going to be okay." As she put her arm around me, I felt myself relax. "We'll get you to the hospital," she promised, explaining that her husband would drive the kids and me in our car while Mary followed in theirs.

Gratefully, I accepted. At the ER, Mary and her husband took the children to the coffee shop for dinner. When I was ready, they were happily waiting for me. As Mary's husband drove me home, I asked, "Where do you live?"

He told me the name of a nearby apartment complex. As we pulled up to my building, I said, "Thank you so much!"

On Christmas morning, I wrote the couple a note expressing my deepest gratitude. A few days later, my letter was returned marked: NO SUCH PERSON AT THIS ADDRESS. I drove to their building, but the manager said, "None of our residents fit your description."

I went back to the ER, but no one remembered the couple. *How could it be?* I wondered. Then it dawned on me: I'd been aided by Heaven that Christmas Eve! Just when we needed them, two angels turned a Christmas calamity into a miracle!

Like Donna, most people who meet angels who have taken human form discover the truth when they attempt to thank them. But Donna's story holds other clues to the angelic couple's Heavenly connections: Since angels are impervious to extreme heat or cold, their light coats and hatless heads (not to mention the lack of snow) showed their Divine origins.

And the second clue comes from Donna herself: The angels' calming energy put her instantly at ease, allowing her to trust them to drive her car and look after her kids! Now Donna and her children know that angels are real—and that's the best holiday gift of all!

The angels say, "We circulate around you in every situation. When we sense your fear, we hover even nearer to your side. In your hours of greatest need, we stand closest. Rest assured that you can lean upon us in any overwhelming situation, and we will support you and your loved ones in all ways."

Angels don't always have wings or white robes. Sometimes they look just like us!

Chapter Two

SENSING THE
PRESENCE OF ANGELS

While they may not talk about it openly, a lot of people have seen angels. One-third of those responding to a poll by *The Skeptic* magazine (a publication devoted to studying paranormal phenomena) reported that they had sighted a celestial being. Surveys in Great Britain and the United States show that between 10 and 27 percent of the general population have had an apparition experience where they saw a departed loved one.

According to a study conducted at the University of Chicago, nearly two-thirds of widows have had such an experience, usually involving their deceased spouse. Investigations at the University of Virginia have concluded that many of these encounters occur during dream time. The Virginia scientists stated that the visitations have a vivid, bigger-than-life quality that distinguishes them from mere dreams.

These scientific inquiries lend credibility to what many people have known or suspected all along: The angels are among us in everyday situations. The following stories illustrate that angels can appear in unusual ways . . . even behind the wheel of a car!

Guiding Us Safely Home

When the weather turns wintry, we rest safe and warm under the loving wings of the angels, as Myrna Holett of Gander, Newfoundland, Canada, recounts:

One sunny Sunday, I took my daughter and her friend cross-country skiing. We were out for hours before I noticed the sinking sun. "Oh no!" I panicked. With no lights and the temperature dropping, we had to get back.

The trail ran along the edge of a golf course, which is where we'd parked the car, and I knew that if we found a shortcut through the trees, we'd be home in no time. But the forest was impassable, and after an hour of searching, we were exhausted, cold, and worried.

Trying not to panic, I prayed, *Please show us a path to the golf course.*

A moment later, my daughter said, "Look!" pointing to a clearing. There, hovering above a hill, was a glowing angel, arms outstretched as if to say, "This way." As the miraculous vision faded, we dashed to the spot where the figure had been, and there was a clear path to the golf course!

Like Myrna, you can call upon Heaven for directions whenever you feel lost. Most of the time, our angels send internal guidance, a hunch, or intuition. But when we're very frightened, they make their guidance—and themselves—visible, as Dorothy Gebhart of Metairie, Louisiana, writes:

One stormy day, I was driving on icy roads when I lost control of my car and started spinning out in the middle of the expressway. Terrified, I closed my eyes, praying, *God, help me!*

Suddenly, my car took off sideways, careening down the embankment, where it stopped. *I'm safe!* I rejoiced. Then reality dawned: My car was in a ditch that was at least a foot deep. To one side stretched miles of highway; to the other, empty, snow-covered fields. *I need help,* I thought.

That's when a Jeep pulled up, and a woman got out, asking, "Can I help you get your car out?"

She was small and slender, and I dubiously asked, "Do you think you can?"

"Sure," she said. "I have a tow chain." And she towed me out in minutes!

"How can I repay you?" I asked.

"Think nothing of it," she smiled. "It's just something I do for God." And as she drove away, I wondered: *Have I just met my guardian angel?*

It surely sounds like Dorothy did. Heaven seems to throw us illogical curves—sending a petite woman to tow us from a ditch, for example, to clue us in that we've received aid from above.

The angels say, "The power of our love for you is stronger than any earthly storms. If you find yourself alone or afraid, simply call upon us for a helping hand."

It doesn't matter *how* you ask for the angels' help. What matters is that you do so.

An Angel Saved Her Life

"I'll never forget the day an angel saved my life," Barbara E. Pleasant of West Columbia, South Carolina, writes:

When I was nine and had finally learned to ride my mother's faded red bicycle, I loved the feeling of flying down Heidt Street hill with the other kids in my neighborhood.

One day as I was pedaling faster and faster, I saw the city bus come into view about half a block ahead. When I pushed on the brakes, trying to stop, I realized that they weren't working!

Frantic, I backpedaled, hoping the brakes would catch—but they didn't, and I knew: *If I don't stop now, I'll slam right into the side of that bus!* "Please, God, help me!" I cried out.

All at once, I thought I saw a flash of white, and I felt a tug on my bike, almost as if someone were pulling it from behind. I slowed down immediately, avoiding the bus in the nick of time! *"Whew!"* I gasped as the bike came to a stop. And I turned, heart pounding, to thank the person who'd saved me . . . but no one was there.

Years later, I've never forgotten that moment on my mother's faded red bike when I realized that my prayer had been answered by the unseen hand of an angel!

The angels responded immediately to Barbara's prayer. They held her bicycle and pulled it out of harm's way. The force was so strong that she assumed she'd see the person who'd stopped her bike. Yet when she turned to thank the person, no one was there, which is a hallmark of angelic intervention.

The angels say, "Rest assured that our power to help you is unlimited. We will do whatever it takes to protect you, as our love is stronger than any physical law of gravity, time, or space."

You and your loved ones are
always watched over by angels.

Heavenly Guides on the Roadway

Angels can perform miraculous feats to protect us from harm, as Patricia L. Miller of San Diego shares:

In 1957, I was driving cross-country to meet my husband, who was stationed aboard the aircraft carrier *Wasp* in San Diego. About 2 A.M., I drove into a heavy rainstorm on Route 60 between Joplin, Missouri, and Tulsa.

The rain was falling so hard that the windshield wipers couldn't clear it, and I realized, *I can't see beyond the hood of my car!* I'd lost sight of the lane markings and, panicking, was afraid to pull over. *If I can't see where I'm going, I could drive into a ditch. But if I keep driving, I might hit another vehicle!* Palms sweating with terror, I cried out, "Oh God! Please help me!"

In an instant, a white Volkswagen Beetle appeared in front of me with its blinker flashing. I could just make out its Oklahoma plates and, heart flooding with relief, I thought: *He must be familiar with the highway. Wherever he's going, I'm going.*

I followed the car to an off-ramp, across an overpass, and into a small gas station.

I parked, turned off my engine, and looked up. The white Beetle was gone! I knew then that the little car had been the answer to my prayer: an angel with wheels instead of wings, sent to guide me to safety.

Most people accept the idea that angels can move physical objects, such as making misplaced car keys reappear. But they can also *create* physical objects, even cars, as Bob Eckman of Burlington, New Jersey, writes:

One rainy night, my wife and I were returning from the movies, driving north on Route 130—a four-lane, 50-mph highway. Visibility was poor, and as we came down a hill, I slowed to go through a large puddle . . . but halfway across, the car's engine stalled.

"Oh no!" I exclaimed, desperately trying to restart it. But the water, much deeper than I'd thought, had covered the tailpipe. Suddenly, in my rearview mirror, I caught sight of two large trucks barreling down the hill, straight toward us!

"They're not slowing down!" I shouted, and we braced for what seemed would be an inevitable crash. All at once, I heard a loud voice: "Put your car in neutral and I'll push you to safety."

I did so, and a white van appeared, placing itself behind us. It pushed us from the highway into a parking lot beside the road, where we sat, very shaken—and very grateful —as the van pulled up beside us.

"You're safe now," one of the two men in the van told us.

"I don't know how to thank you," I said, turning to my wife to say, "Let's give them some money."

But a moment later when I turned back to the window, the men and the van were gone. The parking lot was large and empty, and we would have seen the van leave, but they'd disappeared as suddenly as they'd arrived.

Interestingly, the vehicles that rescued Bob and Patricia were both white. That's the color most often associated with angels' wings and glowing halos.

Both vehicles appeared instantly, and although they seemed solid and real enough, they disappeared once their purpose had been served, a telltale characteristic of angel stories.

The angels say, "Our love for you is so encompassing that it takes on many different forms, from a ray of light to a warm feeling . . . from a gliding butterfly to a white van. Our love radiates like the noonday sun, illuminating every facet of your life."

Pay attention to recurring
themes, as they often contain
Divinely timed messages.

Angel at the Wheel

Car malfunctioning? Your angels could be try-ing to save your life, as Nancy Bebber of Kannapolis, North Carolina, discovered:

> There's this one stoplight in town that always catches me on red. For years, I've played a game with myself trying to get through it on green, but it never happens. Then one night as I approached the intersection, I could tell I was finally going to make it.
>
> Suddenly, from out of nowhere, a bright, beautiful light appeared before my car. I have no words to describe what I saw. It looked like a person surrounded by glowing radiance, the palms of both hands outstretched in a gesture that clearly communicated: *Stop!*
>
> I was so stunned that I sat motionless as the light seemed to engulf my car and stop it—just as another vehicle came flying through the intersection. *That car would have hit me!* I realized, as the light faded away. And I sat there in my stopped car, dumb-founded.
>
> Somehow my stick shift had been placed in neutral, and the hand brake was pulled

straight up. And as the light turned red, a wave of peace washed over me. I began to cry, realizing, *I've had an encounter with an angel.*

Nancy's heart was set on finally beating that stoplight, but her angels were preventing a broadside collision. And they know that sometimes only a "malfunction" will save our lives, as Kathy McInnis of Apple Valley, Minnesota, writes:

One evening I suddenly remembered a prescription that I'd forgotten to pick up and would need later that night. It was 7:45 P.M., and I had 15 minutes to get to the pharmacy before it closed. I jumped in the car and glanced at the rosary hanging from my mirror.

As I came to a busy intersection, I stopped, impatiently waiting for the light to change. *I'll be the first to get across,* I thought, and as soon as the light turned green, I stepped on the gas. But instead of zipping through the intersection, my car sat there, not moving an inch.

I'd barely had time to wonder, *What in the . . . ?* when a huge truck came barreling through the intersection precisely in the path I would have taken. Stunned, I gasped, "Oh my God!" That truck would have hit me directly on the driver's side, and I most certainly would have been killed!

Realizing that I was still pressing the accelerator but my car wasn't yet moving, I lifted my foot and tried again. This time the car moved forward as it always had before. I knew that God sent angels to help people, but now, heart pounding, I grabbed my rosary and thanked Him for sending one to save *me!*

Usually, our angels keep us safe while we're driving by giving us guidance through our thoughts or feelings. However, the women in both stories were in such a hurry that they would have missed their messages, so their Heavenly helpers simply disengaged their cars. Fortunately, no matter how fast we drive, our angels can keep up with us!

The angels can guide you if you
ever get lost while driving. Just ask them
for directions, and trust the feelings
and thoughts that they send you.

Chapter Three

ANIMALS FROM ABOVE

What could be more comforting than the unconditional love of a pet? To many people, their pets *are* angels.

When I (Doreen) was a practicing psychotherapist, I spent a lot of time counseling people who'd lost their beloved animals. Their sorrow was just as deep and painful as those whose family members passed on.

Fortunately, the angels help us overcome grief by giving us comforting signs and messages, as you'll read about in this chapter.

Angelic Animals

Animals can be angels in disguise who support and heal us with their unconditional love, as Lynn Patterson of Mableton, Georgia, writes:

> When my parents started having health problems, family members began staying with them around the clock. It was a time of great worry.
>
> One Friday evening as I drove up to the house, I noticed a little bulldog in the yard. She didn't bark; she just walked with me to the porch. "Where did you come from?" I asked, finding no tags.
>
> In the days that followed, the little dog kept hanging around, and I dubbed her "Lady." Late at night, she'd sit beside me on the porch, and her calm presence helped me open my heart. "It's hard to see Mama and Daddy this way," I'd confide, knowing that she sensed my feelings.
>
> When my mom moved to a nursing home, I shared my sadness with Lady. A few months later, when Mama passed away, I told the dog, "I'm glad that she's finally at peace." The angels sent a furry friend to

remind me of Heaven's love. Lady's calm presence beside me helped me heal.

Then, a few days after Mama's funeral, Lady disappeared. When she didn't return, it occurred to me that she may have been Heaven-sent.

She certainly was! During stressful times, Heaven often dispatches warm, furry angels to soothe and comfort us. We feel safe opening our hearts to animals, and that helps us heal, as Kathy Lynch of Westminster, California, writes:

When I suffered a serious back injury, I went from being an active, busy woman to a virtual prisoner in my own bed. Struggling with unbearable pain, I was unable to participate in the simplest social engagements. Although friends and family stopped by and my daughter took wonderful care of me, I felt so useless!

And one day I lay in bed, weeping. Suddenly, I heard a scratching at my ground-floor bedroom window: It was a little kitten! I could move around the house just a little, so I opened the window and he jumped right in.

Laughing, I said, "Well, hello little fellow." I placed a saucer of milk beside my bed, then lay back to watch him lap it up. When he finished, he leapt onto the bed and nuzzled me. We were nose to nose, and his slanted gold eyes twinkled as he tenderly stroked my cheek with his soft, fluffy paws. Then, resting his head against mine, he fell fast asleep.

My daughter checked but no one had reported a missing kitten. "I guess you're staying," I grinned, and I named him Sammy. Sammy spent most of his time snuggled up with me, and as his gentle purrs warmed my heart, I realized, *My worthiness doesn't come from what I can or can't do. What matters is who I am in God's eyes.*

Animals often arrive just when we need their love and companionship. If you'd like a Heavenly pet, ask the angels to send one to you. They'll find a creative way to introduce a wonderful animal into your life.

Ask the angels to send you
the perfect pet, and they will!

Heavenly Bundle of Love

Sometimes angels have four legs and furry coats. Just ask Patti Reo Williams of Lake Tahoe. She'll tell you that her best friend, Charlie, was Heaven-sent!

Just before my husband, Chuck, died, he looked into my eyes and said, "I know how much you love animals. I'm sorry that I never let you get a cat."

"It's okay," I wept. "I have you to love." But before the sun came up the next day, Chuck was gone.

A few weeks after his death, thinking of his last words, I decided to visit a pet store to see if I could find a cat to soothe my broken heart, but none of the ones there felt like mine. And on the way home, I found myself speaking out loud to Chuck. "You find me the right cat, honey," I said.

No sooner had I stepped in the door when my friend's son called. "Mom says you're looking for a cat," he said. "Well, one just followed me home. Do you want to see it?"

"That was fast," I chuckled at the coincidence. But when he told me, "I live on Williams Drive," a chill ran up my spine:

Williams was our last name. Was it possible that Chuck really *had* sent this cat to me?

The moment I laid eyes on the little ball of fur, I felt an instant connection, and I knew that my husband had indeed helped me find him. In his honor, I named my new friend Charlie. Charlie has been a comfort to me ever since, and knowing that Chuck sent him to me makes his cuddles twice as soothing!

Patti had no doubt that her departed husband had sent her a cat as his gift from Heaven. Animals have such pure and loving hearts that they often work with our angels to help and comfort us—or, as Laralea McLaughlin of Camarillo, California, discovered, to guide us safely home. She writes:

After spending the day on Nantucket Island, my husband, Joe, and I disembarked from the ferry late at night and set off on the mile-and-a-half walk to our hotel. But away from the lighted dock, we found ourselves in total darkness.

I nervously prayed: *God, please send your angels to protect us.* All at once, a massive Saint Bernard came loping toward us. Normally, that would have frightened me, but this dog was clearly friendly, and as Joe and I started to walk, he began trotting along beside us. The entire way back to our hotel, he walked next to us. Then, just as we reached the entrance, he ran off.

"I'm glad he was with us," I said, and it was then that I understood: God had answered my prayers and sent an angel in the form of a beautiful, protective dog!

God certainly did send an angel. How else could you explain his timing? And like other angels, once he'd accomplished his mission, he disappeared.

The angels say, "We send guidance and messengers through the animal kingdom to remind you that love is everywhere and you are never alone."

Pets are angels on Earth, sent to help us feel loved and peaceful.

Angel Kitty

Does your pet bring you comfort? The love of our animals is forever, as Wendy Reed of Clover, South Carolina, discovered:

When my precious 13-year-old cat, Lucky, was diagnosed with cancer, I knew that it was time to end his suffering. With tears in my eyes, I held him close, whispering, "I love you," before putting him in the veterinarian's hands.

My husband made a resting place for Lucky in our yard, where I placed a small cat statue and some catnip. A few days later, I was sitting nearby, missing my kitty and praying, *Please send me a sign that Lucky's okay.*

The day had been completely clear when I'd left the house, but now as I looked up, I gasped: Filling the sky was a beautiful cloud in the shape of a seated cat with angel wings! I watched through tears as the cloud dissipated, feeling blessed beyond words. I knew that Lucky would be fine, with the angels watching over him and me.

Many people see angel-shaped clouds in response to prayers, but a cat-shaped cloud is quite special, especially one with wings! It's clear that Wendy's angels are watching over her and her beloved Lucky.

The angels say, "The love between a pet and a person is pure and Heavenly. It is eternal and remains unbroken even after the animal has transitioned into Heaven. We will bring you signs from all of your precious ones in Heaven. Be open to them, and trust that they are real."

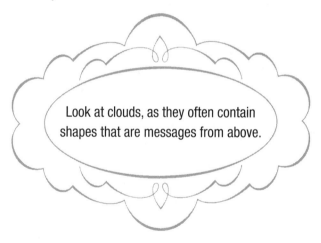

Look at clouds, as they often contain shapes that are messages from above.

The Angelic Dove

Although this story isn't technically about a pet, it does illustrate how birds can act in the capacity of guardian angels. In fact, angels and birds often work together to bring us peace, comfort, and messages of love, as Lorna O'Day of Cherry Valley, Massachusetts, shares in the following story:

Nothing can prepare a parent for the loss of a child. And when my son, Shawn, was killed in a car accident at age 23, my husband, Denny, and I were devastated.

Every day after the funeral, I went to the cemetery to ask God to take care of my son and to ask Shawn to show me a sign that he was okay. Although my heart was breaking, I didn't want to upset my husband and our other children, who were feeling as much pain as I was. So I mostly grieved in private.

One day after reading a card from one of Shawn's friends, I fell apart. Sobbing, I begged God to help me. The next thing I remember, I was out on my deck . . . and I wasn't alone.

There, sitting on the railing just looking at me, was a little mourning dove. He didn't move, even as I approached him. And suddenly, everything in my heart cracked open, and the words began to flow.

"Oh, Shawn," I said. "I miss you so much." I knew that the bird wasn't really Shawn, but there was something about him sitting there so attentively as I poured out my feelings. He felt like the son who'd always seemed to know when I needed a hug. It was easy to believe that God—and Shawn—had sent him to comfort me.

For the next few weeks, the bird visited every day. He'd sit on the deck and I'd pour out my feelings, telling him all the things I wasn't able to share with anyone else.

I never told a soul about my little friend— I knew they'd think I'd lost it—until, one day, I heard Denny talking with someone.

"Who are you talking to?" I asked.

"Well," he said, sheepishly, "you'll think I'm crazy, but there's this bird that comes here every day, and I started talking to him. I feel like he's from Shawn."

Overjoyed, and shocked all at once, Denny and I cried and hugged and shared all our weeks of pent-up sorrow.

I had thought I was alone and a little nuts. But even as the little mourning dove had been helping me ease *my* sorrow, he'd been soothing Denny's heart as well. And now the little bird had led us back to each other.

The bird kept returning for the next few weeks, reassuring us through his constant presence that Shawn was in a wonderful place, and never far from home.

And when, finally, the little bird stopped coming, we knew it was time for us to move on toward healing—together.

Angel signs are always gentle, and what could be more gentle than a dove, the symbol of peace? And what could be more comforting to parents than a creature that echoed their beloved son's qualities of patience and protectiveness?

The angel-dove helped Lorna and Denny gradually heal the worry, anger, and loneliness that are the components of grief. Then it brought them together to heal each other.

Angels often send birds to us as a sign that our departed loved ones are happy in Heaven, and that they still love us very much.

The angels say, "Birds function as earthly angels to let you know that we are nearby and readily available. The next time you see a bird, we ask you to pause for a moment and drink in its beauty and receive the gifts it brings you."

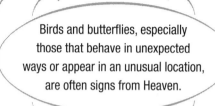

Birds and butterflies, especially those that behave in unexpected ways or appear in an unusual location, are often signs from Heaven.

Chapter Four

PROTECTED
BY THE ANGELS

Our angels are always with us and our loved ones, providing round-the-clock protection. Sometimes they guard us by issuing verbal warnings or intuitive feelings. If we follow this guidance, we're kept safe. On other occasions, the angels use supernatural forces to keep us out of harm's way.

The *Woman's World* readers in the following stories experienced this protection firsthand, and they now know that they're watched over by the Divine. The angels are looking after *you* as well!

Your Child's Guardian Angel

Do you wish your children had angels watching over them? They do, according to Nathalie Flautat of Hallandale, Florida, who writes:

> One evening as I locked up my office, my six-year-old son, Julien, stood watching my secretary cross the street to her car. All of a sudden, he darted after her.
>
> "Stop!" I shouted, racing to catch him. He ran into the road as a car came toward him at full speed. "No!" I screamed.
>
> To my astonishment, Julien's entire body appeared to stop like a freeze frame on TV, barely an inch from where the car sped past him. I rushed over to grab my precious son, tears streaming down my face. I knew that Julien's guardian angel had saved his life!

I have no doubt that the angels intervened just in time to prevent Nathalie's little boy from being struck by that car. Isn't it wonderful to know that they're nearby when we need them?

Ellen Parks of Keansburg, New Jersey, writes about a similar experience:

As a young woman, I babysat for a one-year-old girl named Arlene. One winter, after Arlene had recovered from a bout of whooping cough, her grandmother bundled her into her carriage and sent us out for some fresh air. We'd only walked a few blocks when Arlene started coughing.

I patted her back to clear her airway, but it wasn't working. As she gasped for breath, I panicked. *Oh God,* I prayed, *please help me!*

Instantly, a woman appeared at my side. "Let me try," she said, taking the baby and rubbing her on the back. "She'll be all right now," she reassured me, placing Arlene in the carriage. I turned to thank her, but she'd vanished.

In these stories, the angels had no time to do anything but intervene directly. On other occasions, they inspire, even command, us to help our children ourselves, as Linda Downey of Wellington, Ontario, Canada, writes:

I placed my one-year-old baby girl in her swing in front of our picture window so that she could watch her daddy cutting wood in the yard. I was washing the dishes when I heard a voice say, "Move the baby now!"

There was such urgency to the tone that I couldn't ignore it.

I picked up my daughter, and just as we got into the kitchen, a log came flying through the window, landing right where she'd been sitting!

The voice of Heaven is usually loving and calm, and most people hear it as inner guidance, but when there's a pressing need for the angels to communicate, their voice seems to speak out loud.

The angels say, "We are dynamic teammates with parents, helping to ensure their offspring's well-being. Children are angels upon the earth, and we are never far from their side."

Every day ask the angels
to watch over your loved ones.

The Little Angel

Found an angel figurine? Then look for a real angel—she'll be nearby, as Carol Thomas of New Smyrna Beach, Florida, experienced:

Every day my husband and I take a morning run on Flagler Avenue, a main street in our sweet little town. One time as we jogged along, I caught sight of a shiny object on the ground. "It's an angel ornament," I said. "Or it *was* one . . ."

The little brass ornament was quite squashed, but I liked it and picked it up, saying, "I'll rescue you from this street, and maybe someday you'll rescue me." Dubbing it my "guardian angel," I stowed it in the glove compartment of my car.

A few months later on a rainy afternoon, I was driving home when out of nowhere, another car came slamming into my rear driver's-side door. Shocked and terrified, I gripped the steering wheel as the force of the blow sent my car flipping over the slippery road. Finally, it landed on its side, and I found myself dangling from my seat belt like a marionette!

My car had flipped over at least twice, and I was badly shaken. But checking my body, I didn't seem to be hurt at all! And as emergency workers arrived, freeing me from my seat belt, I eased my foot down to the ground, and there, lying on the smashed glass of my car window, was my little squashed angel!

As tears filled my eyes, I knew what had happened: I'd rescued my guardian angel from the side of the road, and she'd just returned the favor, including making sure that the driver and all the passengers in the car that had hit me were also unharmed! Finding a little angel on the ground showed me that we're never alone.

Carol certainly *was* under her angels' protection. And Heaven found a way to let her know, reminding her that we're always being watched over.

The angels say, "Although we are always nearby, you may not necessarily feel our loving presence. That is why we send you physical signs that you can touch and hold on to. Know that these are symbols of how much we love you."

Whenever you're in a car,
ask the angels to protect you and
all of the other people in *your* vehicle
and in the cars around you.

Safe in the Arms of the Angels

Are you worried about slipping on the ice? Even the weather couldn't stop the angels who were protecting Melissa Mona of Painesville, Ohio, from coming to the rescue! Melissa discovered that when the weather made things dangerous, she got some extra help staying safe.

When angels intervene in emergencies, they do what's needed, but their protection often defies logic. A stranger may help us to safety, then disappear. Or like Melissa, we may be guided by unseen—but very real—hands. She writes:

> I was eight months pregnant and carrying my two-year-old daughter through a parking lot when I slipped on ice.
>
> "Melissa!" my husband shouted. Just as I was about to hit the ground, "something" caught me and pulled me back up!
>
> "How did you do that?" my husband asked, amazed.
>
> "I didn't!" I cried.

Melissa's angels were invisible, but other times they can look just like the kid next door, as Joan M. Voltz of Roseville, Minnesota, writes:

As I walked home from the grocery store one gray winter day, I slipped on some ice. "Ouch!" I winced as I sprawled across the road. I tried to get up, but my ankle was shattered.

"Help!" I cried, but there was no one around. Struggling through the pain, I tried to get to my feet.

Just then a young man appeared. "Can I help?" he asked. He gathered my groceries, then helped me hobble home, where my son led me inside. "Thank Heaven he came along," I said, turning to introduce the kind young man.

But he was gone. That's when I realized that he was my angel!

He certainly was! He was a guardian angel who brought Melissa home to safety.

The angels say, "You may be more aware of our presence in winter, when the icy conditions require our active participation, but rest assured that we are with you always."

No problem is too big—
or too small—for the angels.

Angels to the Rescue!

Angels take whatever form is necessary to save our lives, coming to us through a voice, a feeling, or even a helpful stranger who disappears once we're safe, as Patricia Galanti of Richardson, Texas, shares in this story:

It was a mild night, and I was driving through a four-way intersection when suddenly from the right a car came speeding through the intersection, smashing into my car.

Oh my God! I shrieked as my car was pushed sideways, slamming into a car sitting at the red light on the left. Then, everything went black.

When I opened my eyes, my first thought was *Thank God I'm alive!* Then I realized that I couldn't move!

Yes, you can, "something" told me. And a wave of calm rushed over me.

I sat up, and turning to my left, I was startled to find a woman peering into the shattered driver's-side window. "Turn off the car!" she said.

"It is off," I said, believing that because I couldn't feel the vibration of the engine, the ignition must be off.

"Turn the key," she persisted. I did as she commanded, and when I looked up, she was gone.

That's when I noticed firefighters shouting as they hosed down the street, tow trucks prying the three cars apart, and the roar as the "jaws of life" strained to free the passengers.

Finally, paramedics pulled me from the wreckage. "Good thing you turned off your car," one of them commented. "It was leaking gas. One spark from the ignition and you'd all have been blown sky-high!"

"I just did what the lady told me to do," I said.

"What lady?" he asked. I explained, pointing to where she'd been standing. "That's impossible!" he said. "No one could have stood in that spot before the cars were pulled apart!"

And that's when I knew I'd had a visit from an angel.

The angels knew that Patricia and the other accident victims were in grave peril, so they delivered a short, to-the-point message she could understand and act upon quickly.

Angels often appear at accident scenes. They work hand in hand with earthly rescue workers, and most people don't recognize their angelic identities at all until they inquire about them at the hospital and are told, "No such person works here."

The angels say: "If you are frightened or in danger, we hold your hand (sometimes literally!) and walk with you to safety."

Rest assured that your guardian angels are always with you.

Angel Lights

When you call upon the angels for help, their rescue teams are ready and waiting, as Lynn Anderson of North Miami, Florida, discovered:

I was driving in the rain one evening when a deer ran in front of my car. Swerving, I lost control of the vehicle and went sliding down a steep embankment, finally landing in a deep ravine. I slipped into unconsciousness, then awoke dazed in the cold, dark night.

My car had landed on the passenger side, and the driver's-side door was covered in heavy debris. *I have to get out of here!* I panicked, but I was too weak to open the door above me. "Help!" I cried.

All at once, a calming force took hold of my thoughts. *Turn on the lights,* it guided me. *Yes,* I thought, flipping them on . . . before falling back into unconsciousness again.

I awoke to the sound of voices. Two hunters on their way home around midnight had spotted a light in the ravine and decided to investigate. They pried away the debris and got me out, then drove me to the hospital. "If it hadn't been for that light, we'd never have seen you," they said.

"Thank Heaven you did!" I whispered.

After my recovery, I went to the tow shop. Surveying my damaged car, I couldn't imagine how I'd survived. Neither could the serviceman. "Turning on the lights saved my life," I told him.

"You couldn't have turned them on," he said. "The battery wasn't attached to the car. There was no power."

"But there *was* a light!" I insisted, chills running up my spine. It was then I realized: That illumination had been Heaven-sent! And so were those two weary hunters!

Several miracles saved Lynn:

- She was protected from serious injury.

- She was guided to turn on her light just before two hunters happened to be passing by.

- Plus, the light went on with no power source!

The angels say, "Our protection for you is unlimited, and we are able to bring about what you would call 'miracles' to guard you. To us, they are not, though. They are merely expressions of our love, which is the greatest miracle of all."

If you hear a loving voice give you guidance while you're driving, be sure to listen.

Just Ask

You may not know what's going to happen next, but your angels do! And if you simply ask, they'll throw up a Heavenly barrier to keep you safe, as Ellen Zielke of Crestwood, Illinois, shares:

> Whenever I travel by air, I say this prayer before boarding: *Angels, hold up the wings of this plane. Angels, protect us!* One such day, I recited my usual words, and my husband and I proceeded toward our seats.
>
> Suddenly, I found myself held back by what felt like an invisible barrier. *That's odd,* I thought, trying to press forward. But I simply couldn't take another step. Just then, one of the plane's interior neon lights exploded, shooting a hailstorm of glass right over our assigned seats!
>
> "We could have been cut or even been blinded!" I gasped. But somehow, that "barrier" had protected us.

Ellen assumed that she was praying for the airplane to take off, fly, and land safely, but the angels could see that she needed additional protection.

The angels hear and answer all our entreaties, even the ones that we express as worries, as Barb Kis of Racine, Wisconsin, discovered:

While driving to work, I was consumed with money woes. *How am I ever going to make ends meet?* I worried, pulling into my parking spot. As I stepped from the car, something green caught my eye. "A $20 bill!" I gasped, picking it up from beside my front tire.

The following weekend, I was at the mall when my shoes started to pinch. I bent to loosen them, and right in front of my feet lay a $5 bill! A few days later, I found a wallet in the road. Inside, I found the owner's address. I called him, and when he arrived to claim his possession, he gave me a reward.

The next day, I slid into a pew at church . . . and there, gleaming up from the bench, was a shiny new quarter! All at once, a warm glow filled my heart. I'd gotten the message: Someone in Heaven was looking out for me. I released all my money worries—and you know what? It all turned out okay.

Ellen and Barb both received proof that they were watched over by their guardian angels.

The angels say, "Much of our work is done behind the scenes. Yet we always give you signs to let you know that we are here, and that all is well."

Instead of worrying or complaining, ask your angels to help you with any troubling situation.

Heavenly Rescuers

You're in the hands of the angels! That's what Joan LaChance of Staten Island, New York, discovered one hot summer day at the beach. She writes:

> The summer I was 12, my parents sent me to stay with my mother's cousin, Dolores, and her two daughters on Long Island. At the beach, Dolores cautioned us, "Watch for signs warning against whirlpools, and stay clear of them."
>
> But one day, my cousin Edith and I swam into the dangerous area anyway, as kids sometimes will. Suddenly, the ocean started to swirl and we were caught. Terrified that we'd drown, we both shouted, "Help!"
>
> All at once, I felt a pair of strong arms encircle my waist, pulling me forcefully out of the whirlpool. As I swam back to the beach, gasping with relief, I saw that Edith had also been rescued by a strong man. We fell onto the sand.
>
> "Thank Heaven you're all right!" Dolores cried, hugging us. "I was so afraid you'd drown!"

"We would have," I said, "if it wasn't for those two men who saved us!"

"What men?" Dolores asked. "I saw you swim into and then out of the whirlpool yourselves!"

Edith and I looked at each other in amazement. We asked other people on the beach, but although some had witnessed the incident, no one had seen the men who'd rescued us.

It was only years later that I finally understood what happened: Edith and I had been saved by guardian angels!

Indeed they were! There have been many near-drowning stories with similar scenarios, but this case is unusual because both girls experienced the angelic intervention and could confirm it for each other.

Sandra Johnson of Manteno, Illinois, also had a childhood brush with an angel. She writes:

When I was nine, my best friend and I were playing outside one summer day. In an empty lot near my pal's backyard, we found a huge oak tree with large branches just begging to be climbed. Who could do so faster and higher? We had to know. So up we went, scaling one huge branch after another.

Suddenly, about halfway up, *snap!* As a branch gave way beneath me, I fell, screaming in terror, "Oh God, please help me!"

Just then, I heard a woman's voice whisper, "Fold your arms across your chest." I did as instructed and landed, unhurt, on a patch of cut grass. When I looked for the woman, no one was there.

Alhough Joan and Sandra are grown now, their angels are still with them, as are yours.

The angels say, "When the slightest hint of physical danger arises, we are ready for action, even before you need help."

Angel guidance is always positive and loving, even if it's warning you of danger.

Angelic Protection

When it comes to the safety of children, the angels keep a close eye on those of us behind the wheel, as Patsy Lee Cook of Ripley, Tennessee, shares:

A few years ago, I was working for a home-health-care company, going house to house tending to patients. I encountered many unusual situations, but one will always stand out.

I'd been checking on a patient and chatting with her family members. Among them was a beautiful little girl about three years old.

I completed my tasks, then got into my car. I sat there for a few moments, jotting down notes. I fastened my seat belt, put my foot on the brake, then shifted the car into reverse to back out of the driveway.

I was about to release the brake when suddenly, a sharp voice commanded: "Look to your right!" I did so and was horrified to discover that the girl who'd been inside when I came out was holding on to the door handle of my car!

Relief swept through me as I realized, *If I hadn't heard that voice, I might have killed her!* Later that day, I recounted the story to my co-workers, who were as astonished as I was. A quiet peace came over the office as we all understood that the angels had protected an innocent child and me.

The angels were watching over the little girl; and Patsy, who was acting as a kind of earthly angel by making house calls to care for others, may have been extra sensitive to voices from Heaven.

But you don't have to be an earth angel to hear a warning from the angels. In emergencies, they make sure their directions are loud and clear, as Milton Forbes of Ottumwa, Iowa, shares:

Although this story happened years ago, it's still crystal clear in my memory. I was 27 and working for a large grocery store. At 10 A.M. each day, I'd load my truck and start making deliveries.

Hurrying along my route, I'd come to a stop at each house, kill the motor, jump out with the customer's box of groceries, dash into the house, unload, and rush back to the truck. Then I'd toss in the empty box, start the motor, and sail away to the next house.

On one particular day, I was running through my routine in my usual hurried way, but when I jumped back into my truck and started the motor, I froze stone-cold. Time stood still, and I heard a voice say, "Check the front of the truck."

I immediately turned off the engine, walked around to the front, and gasped: Right there was a small boy on his tricycle. He was leaning against my bumper, looking up at me with a smile.

Chills of cold terror ran through me. I could have killed this little tyke! But something had stopped me. And suddenly, the terror was replaced by warmth and gratitude toward God and the guardian angels who'd protected that boy—and me—from a terrible fate.

There's a lulling energy, the "time standing still" sensation that Milton described, which accompanies angel voices and calms everyone who hears their messages.

The angels say, "A little caution goes a long way in your world, yet there is no need for you to feel afraid while driving, for we are watching over you and those around you (especially children) with vigilance and love. Should the need arise, we spring into action on your behalf."

That car driving slowly in front
of you could be an angel preventing
you from having an accident.

Chapter Five

MESSAGES OF LOVE FROM MOM AND DAD

The bond between children and parents is unbreakable, even after physical death. I say "physical" because the spirit and soul of a person never dies. Neither does the affection between two individuals.

Many people have felt the presence of a departed loved one, and some have even received a visitation. More common, though, are the messages and signs that Heaven sends us to let us know that our family member or friend is happy and deeply cares about us. Of all the angel stories I receive, those about moms and dads are among the most touching. Many parents reach out to their children to say, "I love you," "Please forgive me," and other poignant offerings.

These messages are always a healing balm for grieving hearts, as you'll read in the following stories.

Gifts from Above

Love is so strong that it continues even after we're gone, as Sherie Weber of Moundville, Missouri, reveals:

> My mother was a generous, loving woman —and to my sister, Toni, and me, Mom was also a best friend. So we were devastated when she passed away five years ago. As we sorted through her belongings, I missed her even more.
>
> I was going through a box of old greeting cards that Mom had saved when Toni sighed and suggested, "Maybe we could rent a video and stay here at Mom's for a while." It sounded like just what we needed, but neither of us had any money with us.
>
> *Oh well,* I thought as I opened another card. I gasped: Tucked inside the envelope was a $5 bill! I had to laugh as well as cry. It was as if Mom had been listening in and had said, "Here, girls, go rent your video." So we did, and as we got cozy on the couch, I knew that Mom was there with us, too.

Although it was only $5, that money was a priceless gift for Sherie and her sister. It was a present from Heaven that said, "A mother's love never dies."

Margo Hoornstra of Potterville, Michigan, also received a gift from her mother in Heaven. She writes:

My mom was a constant source of love and encouragement while I was growing up. "Find a penny, pick it up, and all the day you'll have good luck," was one of her favorite sayings. "A dime is ten times the luck, a quarter even more," she'd also remark. As I dealt with life's little problems, I'd always ask her advice, sometimes just to hear her say that things would be okay.

After she died in 1988, I missed her terribly. And when a monumental problem arose, I missed her even more. Just after my husband had to take an early retirement, the place where I worked closed its doors without notice, and I lost my job, too.

Suddenly, our two-income family was a no-income family. Overwhelmed with worry, I took a walk. As I strolled, I began to cry. *Oh, Mom, I wish you were with me now,* I thought. Just then, I looked down, and there on the pavement in front of me was a quarter.

Smiling, I picked it up. And when I looked at the coin's date, I gasped: 1988—the year my mother died!

I knew it had to be a message from Mom letting me know that she'd always be there to love me and encourage my every step.

Margo's mother sent her reassurance the best way she knew how: with a quarter, the coin she'd always used to symbolize abundant luck!

The angels say, "Your family's love for you is so strong that after they are gone, it is often expressed through tokens, signs, and symbols that you can find everywhere you look. Trust that these gifts are in fact from Heaven, because they are."

Ask your angels to send you a sign from your loved ones. You can also request that they help you notice and understand it.

Visits from Heaven

Friends and relatives in Heaven may be trying to send a message of love through a dream, as Suzanne Bodnar of Holbrook, New York, recalls:

One morning last year, I awoke early, scratching my head over the strange dream that I'd just had. In it, I was sitting on a sofa when a woman appeared before me. Touching my face, she said, "My dear, please tell her that I'm all right. Tell her that I love her—that I always have and I always will. Let her know that I hear her and am forever with her."

With that, she turned and walked away toward the most vibrant light I'd ever seen. *Wow!* I thought. It was too real to be just a dream, but I had no idea who the woman was or who her "message" was for.

Still, I grabbed a piece of paper and started scribbling down the details before I forgot them. As I wrote, I suddenly started thinking of my mother-in-law, Iris. Somehow I sensed that the message was for her, and that the woman was her mother, whom I'd met a few times before she'd passed away.

I felt a weird yet strong sense of urgency to call Iris immediately, but it was only 6:45 A.M., so I waited. The feeling didn't fade as the minutes ticked by. And finally, at 7:30, I could wait no longer.

"I hope I didn't wake you," I told Iris, spelling out the details of my dream.

"I can't believe it," she said . . . and as her story unfolded, I couldn't either.

"I woke up early this morning," she told me, "and I couldn't get back to sleep. So I went into the den and sat on my mother's sofa, silently speaking to her. I put my arm around the back of the couch and looked up, asking her to please talk to me or give me a sign. But nothing happened—or so I thought."

Stunned, I asked, "What time was it?"

"Six thirty-five," she said. "I remember reading the clock."

"Amazing!" I told her. "I woke up at 6:38, just three minutes later!"

I gasped. Clearly, this message had been given to me to deliver to my mother-in-law. "But why do you think she came to *me?*" I asked.

"She knew how close we are," Iris said, weeping with joy. "Thank you, Sue, thank you!"

When a loved one visits us during a dream, it's usually to tell us that they're fine, they love us, and not to worry. In this case, Iris was probably too distraught to feel her mother's presence. From her Heavenly perspective, Iris's mom could see the bond between Suzanne and her mother-in-law and chose her messenger well.

The angels say, "Love finds a way. When you set your sights on connecting with caring—whether through a relative, a friend, or us, your angels—you are guaranteed to succeed."

Angels and loved ones often come to us in our dreams. These nighttime visits have very intense emotions that let us know that they're real.

A Father's Eternal Love

Polly Baumer of Florence, Massachusetts, asked for a sign, and the response she got amazed her! She writes:

Spring was my father's favorite time of year. He experienced such joy at the renewal it brings. Five years after his death, when spring came around and I found myself once again missing Dad, I said a prayer asking for some kind of sign that all was well with him and that he knew how much we missed him. I didn't notice anything until a few days later.

While touching up a painting I'd done several years earlier, I thought of Dad again. The painting, depicting a cluster of irises, had always reminded me of him and the flowers he'd planted in the garden of my childhood home.

Suddenly, I found myself wondering again about the sign I'd asked for, and I felt filled with the urge to make the blooms look just right. I searched the Internet for a picture of an iris to study, but none satisfied me. Sighing, I set my brush aside.

Later that day, I was tossing laundry in the hamper when one sock fell behind it. The problem was that our hamper is built-in, and the sock had fallen into the wall. I fished it out using a long-handled back scratcher, and as I pulled it through, I heard the sound of paper moving.

I was intrigued. Our house was built in 1848, and that scrap could have been something really interesting, such as a 100-year-old letter or newspaper.

"Oh, it's an old-fashioned flash card!" I smiled, and looking more closely, I had to laugh.

Printed on the card was the word *flower* and a beautiful illustration of an iris! What a funny coincidence, I thought until I turned the card over . . . and gasped. There on the back was an image of a man with his child and another word: *father.*

Chills running up my spine, I realized, *That card had been in the wall for the 27 years that we've lived in our house!* I don't believe that it's a coincidence that just as I was looking for a picture of an iris, one appeared—especially after I'd asked for a sign from my dad.

It's almost definitely no coincidence. Polly linked the images of irises with her memories of her father, so the angels responded in kind, literally guiding her sock to fall behind the hamper. They knew that the answer to her questions and her prayers lay behind the wall.

The card was Polly's father's way of showing his love. It let her know that he was happy and still cared for her very much.

The angels say, "The messages, signals, and signs that you receive from your loved ones in Heaven are very real. They want you to know how deeply you are appreciated, honored, and cherished."

If you ask your angels and loved ones to help you feel their presence, they will. Trust your feelings, as you can sense the Heavenly beings who are with you.

Mother's Day Messages from Heaven

Our mothers are always close to our hearts, as Roseann Pionegro of Winter Springs, Florida, writes:

> My family spent many happy evenings eating my mom's delicious meals. Our favorite dessert was "peta," a sweet-crusted, layered apple pie. When Dad passed away in 1981, Mom lost interest in cooking, and in 1983, she joined him in Heaven.
>
> Five days later, on Mother's Day, I awoke feeling lonely. I went to her home and surveyed her cookbook collection. She kept her favorite handwritten recipes in between the pages of more than 200 volumes. I found them all, except for the peta.
>
> "Oh, Mom," I said aloud. "Where's your peta recipe?" Suddenly, I had a "feeling." I opened a book that I'd never seen her use, and a small piece of paper fell out: Mom's peta recipe! I was overjoyed. She found a way to tell me that she was still there on this Mother's Day . . . and forever.

Roseann let intuition lead her to what she wanted most: reassurance of her mother's continued, loving presence.

That's also what happened to Judith Risher Christ of White Plains, New York. She shares:

One Mother's Day when I was young, my brother and I bought a beautiful lilac bush for Mom. She planted it in the backyard. For more than ten years, we waited for the plant to bloom, but it never did. Then one early-May day, Mom passed away.

Grief stricken, I prayed for a sign that she was all right. A week later, a single lilac bloomed on the leafy tree, and I knew that this was my sign. Every year since, around Mother's Day that shrub blooms with hundreds of flowers.

The angels have many ways to comfort our hearts. Just ask June Prater of McMinnville, Tennessee, who writes:

When my mother passed away, sadness filled my heart. Each day it ached more. One particularly bad moment, I wept aloud, "Mama, I can't go on much longer without you."

Suddenly, a hummingbird flew up, hovering right before me for a long moment. Then it flew away. I was stunned. My mother had collected these birds! I knew that this was Mama's way of telling me that I wasn't alone—she was right there, just like that little hummingbird.

Your loved ones are never far away.

The angels say, "Simply ask and we will help you feel the love that forever bonds you with your friends and family."

Are you missing your mom?
Ask the angels to send you
a comforting sign of love.

Love Songs from Heaven

Are you missing someone? The angels can help send you a sign of their eternal caring, as Sara Laurance of Ontario, Oregon, discovered:

> Five years ago when I lost my dad, I thought that nothing worse could ever happen to me. But in the two years that followed, my life spiraled into an all-time low. Between financial problems and the end of a 23-year marriage, I was ready to give up.
>
> Then something changed. It was my father's birthday, and I was missing him terribly. I drove to work thinking: *Maybe I should just end it all.* I wept, *Oh, Dad, I wish you were here. You'd know what to say.*
>
> I turned on the radio, and as it came on, the DJ announced, "Here's a special request for a very special person." And all at once, Travis Tritt started singing, "It's a Great Day to Be Alive." That "coincidence" made me feel better.
>
> But before I got home that night, I knew it was no coincidence. I'd heard that same song so many times during the day that I concluded, *Someone's trying to tell me something!* And I knew who it was.

"Thanks, Dad," I whispered as I climbed into bed that night, for he'd saved my life that day. Knowing that he was still there watching over me, I realized: *It really <u>had</u> been a great day to be alive.*

Three years later, whenever I'm down, I still hear that song and it always lifts my heart. Dad found a way to show me that every day is a great one to be alive.

Like Sara's message from her father, Heavenly signs often appear three or more times so that we'll know that they're not mere coincidences. It's wonderful that Sara trusted her feeling that her father had sent the song to her.

And so did Robin R. Mitchell of Indianapolis. She writes:

When I was a little girl in the 1970s, my dad would sing me a song that was popular then called "I Love," by Tom T. Hall, about loving ducks, trucks, trains, and rain. He'd sing and I'd giggle, loving him with all my heart.

As I grew up, Dad and I only grew closer. When he died of lung cancer a few years ago, I was devastated. One Father's Day, I drove to the cemetery and put some flowers on his grave.

"I wish you were here, Dad," I wept. I'd left my car idling with the radio on, and as I climbed back in, I was amazed to hear the old familiar line about loving the little ducks. "Oh, Dad," I cried again, only this time my tears were of joy. I knew that Dad was there with me, telling me that he loved me in a way that I couldn't miss.

Our departed loved ones let us know they cherish us by sending songs that hold special significance.

The angels say, "Music connects Heaven and Earth. Listen closely to the songs you hear today, for they are love letters from above."

If you receive a loving message and think that it's a Divine sign, trust that feeling.

A Gift from Mom and the Angels

Need emergency money? Your angels can help. And just wait until you hear the clever way they solved a financial dilemma for July Astengo of Lynnwood, Washington:

When I was a young girl, my mother used to hide money in "secret" places around the house in case of an emergency. Her cash-stashing habit gave everyone a chuckle— until we needed something. Then Mom would reach into a drawer or behind a piece of furniture and pull out the money to pay for it.

In the years since Mom passed, every now and then we'd find another "stash" and smile, thinking, *Another gift from Mom.* But finally, we were sure that we'd uncovered them all.

Then a few years ago, my sister Kathy's husband was relocated, and the family had to move from our home in Washington State all the way to Texas.

Phone calls kept us close. Still, when my baby was due, I missed my sister so much that I was filled with sadness. And a few weeks before my scheduled C-section, I told her, "I really wish you could be here when the baby comes."

"So do I," Kathy sighed. "I just don't know how we'd ever afford the trip."

"Oh," I caught myself, knowing how much they were struggling. "Don't even think about coming here! Your bills are too important!" And as I hung up the phone, I sent a little prayer, *Please help Kathy's family financially.*

Then, the day before my C-section, guess who showed up at my door? "We'll work out the bills," Kathy said as she hugged me. "This is what's important right now."

I was thrilled to see her, but concern nagged at me, so I continued praying. A few days later, her husband called. "You're not going to believe this," he said. "I knocked a picture off the living-room wall, and there was cash sticking out of the back of the frame. It's a thousand dollars, exactly what we need to cover the bills!"

"Mom!" Kathy and I said at once. And with tears of joy in our eyes, we hugged, knowing that our mother, with her "secret stashes," was still watching out for us.

She certainly is, and so are *your* loved ones. The angels knew that the stash of money was behind the painting and inspired Kathy's husband to "accidentally" find it. You can call on Heaven for anything, including financial help.

The angels say: "Our love for you is so powerful that it allows us to bypass earthly logic to bring you comfort, help, guidance, and protection. Although our methods may seem miraculous, the real miracle is the Divine love that we share with every human being."

Write a letter or have a conversation with your angels or loved ones today—they're always nearby.

Signs from Dad

Dads communicate their love for us in so many ways, even after they're gone, as Debbie Benner of Baltimore shares in the following story:

Growing up, I was a daddy's girl, but I was as stubborn as he was, which sometimes caused little spats. Whenever this happened, Dad's way of smoothing things over was to find a bird feather on the ground for me. Throughout my childhood and into my adult years, it just seemed to fix everything.

Then, when I was in my late 20s, my father became gravely ill. Sad and worried, I'd take walks by myself, and each time I'd find a feather! And when Dad passed away, the feathers kept coming.

In the weeks following his funeral, I found some of the most colorful ones I've ever seen. They showed up in the oddest places, often appearing out of thin air before my face, but always when I needed them most. I've kept all of my father's feathers from Heaven.

To this day, whenever I'm feeling down, I find another loving gift of this kind from my father.

Throughout her life, Debbie's father's feathers were a symbol of his love for her. So it was only fitting that he and the angels chose to place especially colorful ones in unusual locations to ensure that Debbie would have no doubt about their message.

The angels often send familiar personal objects to comfort and reassure us. They even pass us notes, as Renee Lukawszek of Toledo, Ohio, writes:

> I was devastated after losing my dad in a car accident. I didn't get a chance to say "I love you" or good-bye. He was just gone.
>
> A week after the funeral, I returned to my job in the children's department at a retail store. Seeing all the kids with their dads was hard for me. All I wanted was to be with mine, too.
>
> That day a woman appeared in the store. I hadn't seen her walk in—I would have noticed, since there were no other customers around.
>
> "May I help you?" I asked. She told me that she had some clothes to return. "Do you have a receipt for the purchase?" I asked.
>
> "Yes," she said, but she seemed hesitant to give it to me. "It's just that there's a personal note on the back of it," she explained.
>
> "I only need it to process the return," I said. "I'll give it right back." I turned to the

register and did her return. I stapled the receipts together, but when I turned to hand them back to her, she was gone. *That's odd,* I thought.

I began to slip the papers into my register drawer when something told me, "Look at the other side of the receipt." My eyes went wide with shock: There on the back was a note written in my father's handwriting. Tears filled my eyes as I read, "I love and miss you. Dad."

Gripping the precious receipt, I silently thanked the mysterious woman who'd brought it to me, knowing that she'd been Dad's messenger of love.

Angels can take on human form when necessary, and it's very likely that the woman in Renee's store was one of these "incarnated angels." The signs; her sudden appearance and disappearance; and the message she brought, a loving letter to Renee in her father's own handwriting, all confirm this.

The angels say, "Just as the sun shines down to warm your body, allow our caring to warm your heart. Your loved ones who have passed on are attended to by us, and they are happy and safe. If ever you need reassurance from someone, be it a person on Earth or in Heaven, call upon us, and we shall do the rest."

Ask the angels for a loving sign
from your father, and then notice the
messages that begin to appear.

A Christmas Visit from Dad

In times of worry, our guardian angels and loved ones stand ready to help, protect, and support us, as Shantel Bothwell of Twin Falls, Idaho, experienced:

It was Christmastime 2002, and instead of feeling holiday cheer, I was a nervous wreck. The next morning my new husband and I would be in court to finalize custody papers with the birth father of my 22-month-old son, Dylan.

The thought of standing in a courtroom had me on edge. *How I wish Dad could be here,* I thought as I stepped into my parents' house in California. But sadly, he'd passed away three years earlier.

Later that night, I woke to find Dylan standing beside my bed. "Mommy, walk," he said, tugging at my hand.

"It's too late," I yawned, tucking him back into bed. "We have to wake up early tomorrow."

But a moment later, he was back. "Walk. Walk," he repeated. Finally, I gave in. He led me down the hall to the family room.

"Do you want to sleep in here?" I asked. Picking him up, I sang to him in front of the darkened Christmas tree.

Suddenly, Dylan stretched his arms toward the tree behind me, calling, "Grandpa Angel!" *What?* I thought, spinning around just as three beams of light flashed across the wall. Then Dylan wiggled to be put down, saying, "Bed now."

I'll never know what Dylan saw that night. But with tears in my eyes and a heart filled with peace, I knew Dad was there to comfort me, and that everything would be fine in court the next day . . . and it was.

But don't stop reading yet, because there's more: Earlier this year, I was reading *Woman's World* when I came across the "Feathers from Heaven" story. *This reminds me of our "Grandpa Angel,"* I thought with a smile as I read the accounts from people who'd received signs from deceased loved ones.

At the end of the story, Doreen wrote: "You, too, can ask for a sign from a departed loved one. Simply pray, speak, or write your request." And although I wasn't sure that I'd get one, I asked my father for a sign.

I turned the page, but something kept pulling me back to that "My Guardian Angel" column. *Maybe I should send my story in,* I thought. Then I saw *Woman's World*'s address: 270 Sylvan Avenue. Chills ran up

my spine. Sylvan was my father's first name!
I had my sign.

Worry and stress can shut down our awareness of Heaven's loving presence, but children are especially attuned to the angels. In their openhearted state, they easily recognize Divine guidance, so the angels prompted Dylan to deliver their message of comfort.

After that, Shantel was more open to receiving assistance from her guardian helpers. She trusted her own inner guidance and quickly received the sign she'd asked for, reaffirming her connection to her father and the angels watching over her and her family.

Babies and children are very attuned to seeing and hearing angels because they're so open-minded and filled with faith.

Chapter Six

HEAVENLY SIGNS

Don't you wish that angels would write their messages in plain English and hand them to us to read so that we could clearly understand their guidance? For some reason, though, God's plan must involve humans meeting them halfway.

One of the main ways in which Heaven communicates with us is by sending us signs—messages that we see or hear with our physical senses. Usually, the angels repeatedly send the same one until we understand its significance. If you see or hear something three or more times, pay attention because it's probably a message from above.

The angels send us signs in the form of songs that we repeatedly hear. Notice the lyrics, as they may contain a message. Or perhaps the tune itself holds special sentimental value and is linked to a particular departed friend or relative. In this way, you're receiving a love song from Heaven.

Other angel signs include flickering lights, moved objects, finding coins or feathers, or seeing rainbows or angel-shaped clouds. Heaven communicates with us in countless ways, as you'll read in the following stories.

If you want a sign from your angels or a departed loved one, just ask! It's best not to specify which type you want . . . let Heaven surprise you. But do ask for assistance noticing, trusting, and understanding the signs. Remember: Your angels want to help you with *everything*, including decoding seemingly cryptic messages.

Signs of Love

Do you keep finding loose coins on the street? If this happens a lot, it may mean that someone you love is trying to get in touch with you, as Jeannette McDermott of Stuyvesant, New York, writes:

"Why do you need all these rubber bands?" I'd often ask my husband, Peter.

"They might come in handy one day," he'd laugh.

I failed to understand his odd obsession, but I didn't really mind—until he filled a whole kitchen drawer with the stretchy bands! Exasperated, I threw them all away. Peter just chuckled and started collecting them again.

Then, a year ago Peter passed away. Heartbroken, I thought: *No more rubber bands, no more laughter, and no more love.*

A few weeks later, while walking with my granddaughter, I found two rubber bands on the sidewalk. "Look," I said, pointing. A friend had told me that departed loved ones often send dimes to say, "I'm still with you." Couldn't they also send . . . rubber bands?

So as I bent to pick them up, I said, "Maybe they're a sign from Grandpa."

"Oh, Grandma," my granddaughter said, "those rubber bands come with everyone's newspaper." *Maybe she's right,* I sighed. But later that day, as I stepped out of my car, there beside my foot was a shiny dime—and next to it, a rubber band!

My heart overflowing with joy, I knew: *Peter is sending me a message!* In the days that followed, I started finding rubber bands and dimes everywhere: on chair cushions, in my car, even in my pockets!

And now instead of discarding the rubber bands, *I'm* the one collecting them as comforting reminders of my husband's love. Now I know that the affection I shared with Peter will last for all time.

What a beautiful illustration of the enduring power of love. As Jeannette's friend told her, Heaven often sends coins to comfort us. So when Jeannette's husband paired a dime with his favorite collectible, he knew it would tell his wife, "These are real signs from me. Trust them."

You can ask for a sign, too! Just let Heaven choose which one to send. Your intuition will tell you if it's real, but if you're still doubtful, just request more signs.

The angels say, "We delight in our interactions with you. Some signs you see, some you hear, and others you feel within your heart. All are equally significant. The more you know that we are real and that we love you, the more your life becomes healthy, peaceful, and joyous."

The angels are here to help you heal your life, and they want you to ask for help!

Rainbows and Roses

How can you be sure it's really a sign? Well, Julie Miller of Hudson, Ohio, asked for one and got a deluge of them! She writes:

I was very close to my grandmother, who suffered from diabetes and heart disease. So when her condition worsened, Grammy and I discussed how she'd send me a sign from Heaven when her time came.

"How about a rosebush?" I suggested.

But Grammy was concerned that she wouldn't be able to send me one in the winter, so we settled on a rainbow as our personal sign.

On the day of her funeral, I was working in my garden, trying to take my mind off missing her, when suddenly it began to rain . . . but only on me! *This can't be!* I thought, looking around. But it was—no other part of the backyard was getting wet! And when I looked up, there it was: a huge, bright rainbow arcing across the sky!

In disbelief, I wept tears of joy, for Grammy had sent me a sign! And that wasn't the only one she'd dispatch! Her next sign arrived on the way to the doctor's office. Prenatal testing had shown a possible problem with my baby, and I silently prayed, *Please let everything be all right.*

Suddenly, my attention was drawn skyward, where I saw a double-arced rainbow. Later that day, I learned that my baby was fine—but Grammy's rainbow had already told me that! A few weeks later, I noticed a thorny stick taking root in my garden. I had no idea what sort of plant it was. Curious, I let it develop.

The next summer, a full bush grew and blossomed with wild roses. *But where had it come from?* I wondered. There were no roses in my garden. Then, laughing out loud, I realized: *It's from Grammy!* She had found a way to send me rainbows and roses!

Julie and her grandmother couldn't have chosen two better signs! Rainbows, a sign of hope, and roses, timeless expressions of love, are often used by the angels and our departed loved ones to say, "I love you," "Please don't worry about me," or "I'll always be with you."

And that's just what Grammy's signs told Julie. "Her signs from Heaven left no room for doubt," Julie comments.

The angels say, "We continually bring you messages of love. Some of them you detect, but others go unnoticed. Even when you do not observe or trust the signs, you always feel them deep within your heart, reminding you that you are never alone and are always deeply loved."

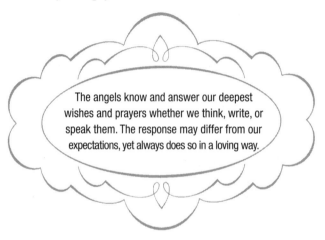

The angels know and answer our deepest wishes and prayers whether we think, write, or speak them. The response may differ from our expectations, yet always does so in a loving way.

One Last Smile . . .

Love lasts forever! Lisa DiGenova just wanted to see her husband's smile one more time. What happened next will amaze you:

When my husband, Phil, died suddenly at age 42, I was overwhelmed. I'd met him when I was 18, and we'd been together for the last 18 years. I didn't know anything about being on my own. How would I pay the bills? Could I raise our children (two teens and a toddler) alone?

Shortly afterward, I was celebrating our son's 14th birthday without Phil, and the reality of being a single mother only made me miss him more. I tried to stay cheerful, but all day long I found myself praying, *Oh, Phil, if I could just see your smiling face one more time.*

That night as we gathered around the kitchen table to sing "Happy Birthday" and cut the cake, my son started snapping Polaroid photos. He was watching one develop when he gasped. "Mom," he said, voice trembling. "Look!"

I stared, baffled and teary-eyed, as there in the photo, clear and unmistakable, the

119

image of my husband came slowly into focus! Phil stood beside our daughter's high chair, arms folded, grinning. Seeing his beautiful smile made my heart melt with love.

"Your dad's here!" I whispered, sharing the miraculous image with the children. Awestruck, weeping, we passed the picture around. Soon Phil's image began to fade, but not before everyone had seen him. When it vanished, leaving behind a little bright spot on the photo, I knew that this beautiful gift from Heaven had turned our lives around.

I no longer felt overwhelmed and hopeless. Now that I knew Phil was still with us, I was sure that we'd be fine . . . and we are: I became a preschool teacher; and the children are healthy, happy, and thriving. My prayers were answered with a smile.

When a loved one passes away suddenly, without a final good-bye and an "I love you," we feel unsettled and incomplete. We worry if he or she is happy in Heaven. Like Lisa, we may even stop living our own lives fully.

Although Phil's smile appeared only briefly, it was enough to provide the healing that Lisa needed. It affirmed that her husband was happy and knew that she would be, too. There are many reports of angelic appearances in photos: sometimes as orbs of light; other times, as in Phil's case, with recognizable faces and bodies. Remember that the angels and our loved ones want us to feel loved and safe.

The angels say, "If your heart grieves for a lost loved one, think of happy memories you have shared. Your love exists eternally in both of your souls. Call upon us if you need a physical sign of this love, and stay aware. Messages can occur in so many ways."

Ask the angels to appear in your photographs, and then notice the orbs of light and other distinctive shapes in the pictures you take.

Answered Prayer

The angels send clear signs to let us know that our prayers are heard, as Catherine Policastro of Whiting, New Jersey, shares in the following story:

When my oldest son, Jeff, told me that his doctors had found a quarter-sized spot on his lung, I was terrified. Jeff, 28, had been a smoker since his teen years, and although his doctors played down their concerns, they were 90 percent sure that it was cancer.

I immediately began asking God to spare him. A few days before Jeff was scheduled for surgery, I was praying when an image appeared before me: a semicircle of angels in long white gowns. One stepped forward and showed a vision of my son on the operating table, surrounded by seven doctors. Behind them stood the circle of angels, conveying to me that they'd be there with him through the surgery.

I awoke from this vision feeling comforted and hopeful. Still, on the morning of the surgery, I hit traffic on my way to the hospital and arrived feeling frantic. "The operation's over," my daughter-in-law informed me. "It wasn't cancer!"

I listened in amazement as she told me the details of Jeff's surgery. There had indeed been seven doctors in the operating room—seven *astonished* doctors, for whatever the spot on Jeff's lung had been, it had somehow destroyed itself. The surgeons called it a miracle, and I knew that it was.

Heaven showed Catherine a vision of seven doctors and the angels who would help them care for her son, which lent comfort to a worried mom. And later when she learned what had actually happened in the OR, she had no doubt that her vision had come true.

Angel signs don't always come directly to us. Sometimes angels send a sign through a relative, friend, or even a co-worker, as Karen Prescott of Erie, Pennsylvania, writes:

I knew that I'd missed my co-worker (and best friend) Lori's birthday while I was recovering from knee surgery. As soon as I was able to hobble around on crutches, I bought her a pretty calendar as a gift.

But before I had the chance to give it to her, Lori died in a car accident. Oh, the emptiness I felt—and guilt that I'd missed her birthday.

A few days later, Jack, another co-worker, pulled me aside. "I had a dream about Lori," he said. "She gave me a message for you: *Tell Karen, 'Thanks for the calendar.'*"

I didn't know what to say—I hadn't told a soul what I'd bought for Lori. Tears filled my eyes as I realized that she had found a way to let me know that she'd appreciated the gift . . . and our friendship.

Like Karen, many bereaved people feel remorse that they didn't do enough for their loved ones. I'm guessing that this guilt prevented her from directly receiving the message that Lori and the angels wanted to convey to her. So they delivered it through a co-worker.

The angels say, "We constantly send you signs of our ever-present love—some of which you notice, and some you do not. Yet the effect is the same whether or not you are aware of the signs. You are continuously enfolded in angels' wings, wrapped safely in Heaven's love."

Pay attention to your dreams
and inner visions, for they often contain
messages from the angels.

Our Son's Dream Car

· ·

When those we love leave us, our hearts long for signs that they're at peace. And sometimes we find these signs in unusual places, as Susie Snider of Port Washington, Wisconsin, shares:

When our 32-year-old son, Timm, passed away suddenly from heart arrhythmia after a 90-minute soccer game, my husband, Don, and I were devastated. And a year later, we were still filled with sadness. One day we went to the park, where we walked together, talking, crying, and remembering Timm. And before we left the park, we prayed for a sign to let us know he was okay.

It was on our way home that my husband noticed a silver BMW, our son's dream car, quickly approaching in the rearview mirror.

"Look at this guy!" he exclaimed, drawing my attention to the car as it pulled up alongside and quickly in front of us. It was then that we noticed the license plate that read: *IM OK 7*. The car stayed in front of us for a minute or two as we sat stunned, gaping at the message.

"Timm's soccer number was 7!" I recalled.

"I know," Don nodded, tears in his eyes. A moment later the car sped away as quickly as it had appeared.

Susie's husband could have dismissed the silver BMW as just another car. But its connection to his son, and to the prayer he and his wife had just offered, made him pay attention.

Sometimes the angels don't wait to be asked to send signs of comfort—dispatching rainbows, angel-shaped clouds, birds, butterflies, and flowers to ease a grieving heart. And if we miss those signs, they send more personal ones (a song tied to our lost loved one, for example) until we get the message.

The angels say: "It is normal to grieve when a loved one crosses over to our side. Your loved one feels your pain intensely. Therefore, your greatest gift to him or her is to heal your heart. We send you signs to reassure you that your loved one is at peace."

Notice license plates and bumper stickers, because they often convey personal messages from Heaven.

Heavenly Signs of Love

It's one of life's great mysteries why some children are taken home to Heaven before their parents. Yet the angels find ways to assure us that these kids are in their loving care, as Annette L. Adams of San Marcos, California, discovered:

> As autistic children will often do, my daughter Stacy would fixate on simple objects, spinning pot lids and twirling fat rubber bands on the floor. But her favorite object was a small, dark blue ball. We were certain that her little blue "friend" helped calm her fears about the daily seizures that she experienced.
>
> Tragically, one day a seizure claimed my Stacy's life. Devastated, I searched everywhere for her little blue friend, wanting her to have it when we laid her to rest. But I couldn't find it anywhere. In the 22 years since Stacy passed away, my husband and I have moved several times. We'd step into each new home thinking that it would bring us happiness, only to find that it didn't.
>
> We missed Stacy, as well as our other daughter, Michele, who was now grown with

a family of her own living hours away. So last year, when we were finally able to relocate closer to them, I found myself hoping: *Maybe this home will bring us happiness.*

Just days after moving in, while walking through the backyard, something caught my eye: a little blue ball! I smiled, picking it up. But this wasn't just any ball—I recognized it as the exact same one that Stacy had loved! Suddenly, joy filled my heart and tears flowed, for I knew that Stacy and the angels were telling me that we'd finally found our happy home, living near her sister and enjoying our grandchildren every day.

Annette's daughter had found great pleasure with her little blue ball. So the angels chose it as a sign that Annette had finally found her home.

The angels often select personally meaningful objects such as the little blue ball to ensure that we receive their messages of love, as Mary Ann Doine of Haven, Wisconsin, writes:

On December 6, 1967, my 20-year-old brother, John, was killed in Vietnam. My parents were devastated, and the American flag became an important symbol to them. They always made sure that the one on Johnny's grave was never tattered.

Years later, as my mother lay dying, my thoughts turned to Johnny. *Please don't let Mom be alone,* I silently begged him. *Be with her when she comes to Heaven.*

Driving home after her funeral, I prayed for a sign that she was okay. And as I turned the car into the driveway, my eyes grew wide: There, sticking out of the ground in the middle of the garden bed that I'd just finished clearing, was a little American flag!

I burst into tears of gratitude and joy, praying, *Thank you for this sign letting me know that you and Mom are all right.*

The little flag was a symbol of love and comfort in answer to Mary Ann's prayer. It was Johnny's way of saying, "Don't worry, Sis. I'll be here for Mom."

Each of us has at least
two guardian angels personally
assigned to us for our entire life.

Ask Your Angels and They'll Answer!

The angels are eager and ready to help everyone, as Angela Gambs of Uhrichsville, Ohio, shares in the following story:

I dated the same man from ages 15 through 24. Josh and I were engaged, bought a house together, and then had a terrible breakup. Still, we shared a bond that I thought would last forever. However, that dream was shattered in 2003 when he tragically passed away.

Two years later, I still hadn't completed the grieving process, and I decided to write him a letter. I poured my heart out onto the page, writing: "I will always love you." Then I asked for a sign to let me know that he believed this.

Later that day, I picked up the August 2 issue of *Woman's World*. There, I discovered a story in which a woman's mother sends her a message of love through a special song. And when I read the words "I love you a bushel and a peck," I gasped: That's the song Josh and I had sung to each other every day! I had my sign!

How wonderful that Angela received a clear sign from her loved one after reading the "My Guardian Angel" column. The angels have told me that this is one of their platforms for comforting many people.

And it's working, as Barbara Garneau of Lowell, Massachusetts, shares:

> On the day of my surgery, I put my wedding band and three diamond-and-gold bracelets into a small pink purse for safe-keeping. But when I returned home from the hospital, the purse was gone.
>
> Now I wouldn't be able to pass my treasures down to my granddaughters as I'd planned! I cried. Three months later I was reading the column and decided to ask the angels for aid, praying: *Please help me find my jewelry.* Not ten minutes later, "something" told me to pull out the table beside my armchair . . . and there, wedged in a corner, was the little pink purse!

Barbara took the two essential steps when calling on the angels: (1) She asked for help; and (2) she followed the guidance she received, the "feeling" to look behind the table—and there was her jewelry!

The angels often lead us to meaningful treasures, as Janis L. Huston of London, England, writes:

My mom, who passed away two years ago, had been my best friend. As an American living in London, I'd counted on my mother's calls to help me feel connected. Mom had introduced me to *Woman's World* a few years back, and I'd bought a subscription so that I could get it in the U.K.

And when I read the story about the mother who'd collected nickels, I had to smile. Mom had collected coins, and since her death I'd been finding them whenever my husband and I would take our walks. Of course they were always British ones.

But after I read your story, I found a shiny American nickel! In the seven years that I'd lived in London, I'd never found a U.S. coin. I picked it up, filled with joy, for I knew that Mom was letting me know that she would always be there.

That found nickel was a Divinely arranged sign—just what Janis needed to know that her mom was still with her! "Thanks to *Woman's World,* I got an angel message!" she says.

Want a sign from the angels?
Just ask for one . . . then keep your
eyes open and trust what you see.

A Holiday Gift of Light

Our angels know that although the holidays are joyous, they can also be stressful, so they find ways to comfort us—as Kathleen Mulcahy of Sun City Center, Florida, found out:

Three years ago when my husband, John, passed away, I missed him terribly, especially at night. In our 58 years together, we'd discussed the idea of life after death, and we'd promised each other that whoever went first would send the other a sign to show that all was well.

But after John died, I only felt grief. A few days after his passing, I was having a particularly bad night, sitting in the dark of our bedroom, weeping. Suddenly, my little lamp flickered on, flooding the room with illumination.

That's strange, I thought. The little light reminded me of our promise to "stay in touch," and my heart filled with love. It would be just like John to come when I'm hurting. *Maybe he's trying to send me a message,* I thought. For a few days, nothing more happened. Then, the light flickered repeatedly.

"John, is that you?" I whispered—and a few times, remarkably, the lamp flickered as if in response. *It is John!* I thought, and my loneliness began to lift. As the weeks passed, John kept making his presence known. I'd leave the house, turning off all the lights, and when I'd return, the little lamp would be on to welcome me home.

And I wasn't the only one John greeted with lights. When my granddaughter (who'd been very close to him) visited, the lamp popped on as if to say, "Hello!" Still, I knew that even with my husband's "bright" presence, the holidays wouldn't be easy without him.

As I decorated the tree on Christmas Eve, after draping the strings of lights on, I found myself speaking out loud to him as if he were really there: "John, I'm going to turn the lights off now so that I can put the ornaments on."

As I set each one in place, overcome with memories of Christmases past, I brushed away a few tears. I hung the last glittering ball and suddenly, on came the lights!

"Oh, John," I wept. "Thank you for staying with me!" His lights let me know that our love didn't end with his passing. And that's helped me move on and no longer feel alone.

Our loved ones don't stop loving us or wanting to be with us after they're gone. And making lights flicker is one of their favorite ways to let us know they're with us.

The angels flicker them, too. And there are other signs of their presence: a featherlight sensation against our cheek, a meaningful song, or a familiar scent. Almost anything can be one if it has significance for us. And as our hearts and minds open to signs, we receive more!

The angels say, "We are helping with your holiday prayers by bringing you peace in deeply personal ways. Feel our presence and know with complete certainty that you are protected and loved."

Your departed loved ones are happy in Heaven, and they're in the protective care of angels.

ANGELS FINDING LOST OBJECTS

Nothing is hidden or truly lost to the angels because they can see the location of everything and everyone. Because we have free will, though, we must first ask them for help in finding lost objects (or people or pets) before they can intervene.

You can ask the angels silently, aloud, or in writing, as the form or verbiage of your request doesn't matter. What *does* count is that you ask.

After requesting their help, the angels will assist you in one of two ways:

1. The first is through directing you to the location of the lost object. You'll receive this guidance as a thought or idea, a vision, words that you hear, or strong feelings. It's important that you follow these leads, as they're the road map to finding what you're looking for.

2. The second way that the angels help is by bringing the object to you. You won't see it float through the air or instantly appear before your eyes, but you *will* find the item in a location where you've already looked several times before.

Either way, you'll know that the angels have helped with the success of your search, as the *Woman's World* readers in the following stories experienced.

Nothing Is Ever Lost to the Angels

. . . .

Have you misplaced something precious? Why not ask the angels to help you find it? From their Heavenly perspective, they know just where it is, and they'll find a way to return it to your loving care.

The angels are great detectives! When we ask for their help, they lead us to the item, as Lynda Jessup discovered:

> My sister, Patsy, was confined to a wheelchair after contracting polio at age 11. Patsy's limited movement didn't stop her from developing her artistic talents, one of which was creating beautiful beaded jewelry. Three years ago, she made me a stunning necklace-and-earring set, which I treasured, but somehow I lost one of the earrings.
>
> When Patsy died suddenly a year later, I was inconsolable. *Please send me a sign that she's okay,* I prayed. One morning, the strangest thought popped into my mind: *Go into the closet and get out the lingerie bag.* I couldn't remember the last time I'd used that bag, but I had to dig it out.
>
> Dumping the contents onto my bed, my breath caught in my throat: There, trapped

in the threads of a little doily, was my missing earring! Joy rushed into my heart as I sensed my dear sister's presence.

Through happy tears, I said out loud, "Oh, Patsy. Thank you for helping me find this. And thank You, God, for my sign." On that day, my heart began to heal.

Sometimes we shrug off our angels' guidance, which comes in the form of hunches. But when Lynda followed those gut feelings, she found her lost treasure—along with the certainty of her angels' presence.

The angels say, "Nothing is ever truly lost, but merely misplaced. We can guide you to find anything if you let us."

Archangel Chamuel (pronounced *sham-you-el*) is wonderful at finding lost objects. Call upon him if you ever misplace anything.

Reunions with Heirlooms

Can't find something? Your angels know where it is. From their Heavenly perspective, they can see everything . . . and if you ask, they'll direct you straight to it, as Alesia Vassallo of Lansdale, Pennsylvania, writes:

Whenever I'm feeling nervous before a social event, I put on a cherished pair of earrings that my mom gave me. Somehow having them on makes me feel wrapped in my mother's reassuring presence.

So last year I wore them to a wedding, and the day turned out great. But later as I undressed, I realized that I'd lost an earring! *Please help me find it,* I prayed as I searched the car and house. My husband called the country club, but it was no use.

The next day, hoping to cheer me up, my husband offered, "I'll clean out your car." A few minutes later, he returned, grinning, with my latest copy of *Woman's World.* "Look what I found," he said. And there, actually stuck to the "My Guardian Angel" page, was my earring!

"It was just like this when I found it!" he marveled. Amazed and grateful, I thanked my angels for the reminder that I'm always protected.

You *are* always protected. Alesia's angels placed her earring on the "My Guardian Angel" page as a reminder of that fact. I've received hundreds of stories from people who, like Alesia, asked the angels for help with finding lost jewelry, keys, and wallets and always got what they were looking for!

Just ask Martha Hood of Cottondale, Alabama. She writes:

Farris was my friend for more than three decades. A few years ago, he gave me a special bracelet and told me, "This is a reminder that I'll always be there for you." After he died, wearing the bracelet seemed to ease my sadness.

Then, last month after lunch with a friend, I realized, *My bracelet is gone!* We looked everywhere, but it was no use. "I wish Farris could tell me where it is," I sighed.

Suddenly, something told me, "Look down at your feet." I did so—and there, caught in a crack between the sidewalk and a wooden step, was my bracelet! I started crying because I knew that my special friend was still there for me . . . only now he was one of my guardian angels!

The angels say, "We are happy to reunite you with anything that seems to be lost. This is especially true with an heirloom, as the love you feel for the person who bequeathed it to you forever links you to that individual and to the object. No matter how long the item has been missing, we will help you find it."

Instead of stressing over a misplaced item, take a moment to ask your angels for their help in locating it.

Whatever You're Looking For,
the Angels Can Help You Find

Sandra L. Collingridge of Pembroke, Massachusetts, was touched by a *Woman's World* story and felt inspired to reach out to her angels:

> Late last fall when my mother gave me a copy of *Woman's World,* I was totally captivated by the "My Guardian Angel" column. And when I read the story about the woman who'd misplaced some jewelry, I was inspired!
>
> You see, 15 months earlier my mother had misplaced her diamond engagement ring and wedding band. We'd all been preoccupied with my father's surgery, and although we searched everywhere, the rings were nowhere to be found.
>
> Mom was terribly upset about losing the precious symbols of their marriage. And when Dad passed away from complications, the loss of the irreplaceable rings was even more painful. We'd all but given up on finding them.
>
> But when I came upon your story, a tiny spark of hope flickered back to life. *If*

the angels could help that woman recover <u>her</u> jewelry, I thought, *why not ours?* So I asked, *Angels, can you help us find Mom's rings?*

Two days later, my mother called. "I found my rings!" she rejoiced.

Astonished, I asked, "Where were they?"

"In the toe of a brand-new pair of socks!" Mom said.

Socks? I laughed. And although the location didn't make sense, I was deeply grateful, for I knew just who'd led Mom to her rings.

Months later, I'm still amazed by the clever and quick way the angels answered my prayers. I'm so grateful to Doreen and to *Woman's World.* Perhaps this story will inspire someone else to ask their angels for help!

Sandra's father and the angels most certainly had something to do with this event! And perhaps the jewelry was "placed" in that unusual location so that the family would be certain that finding it was no accident. The angels are happy to retrieve anything for us. What matters is that we ask, speaking our request out loud, praying silently, or writing it down.

The angels say: "Of course we are happy to reunite you with anyone or anything that is a symbol of love for you. Nothing to which you are attached can ever truly leave you. We await your invitation to become involved in the 'search party' as you become increasingly open to working with our help."

Your angels can assist you in finding anything you're looking for, including objects, a wonderful romantic partner, or a great job.

Chapter Eight

ANSWERED PRAYERS

All prayers are heard and answered by the angels, since that's their infallible mission. However, we may not immediately recognize these responses because they appear in ways that differ from our expectations.

So having faith and an open mind are essential to enjoying the gifts that the angels bring our way, as the following stories illustrate.

The Rainbow Bear

When we ask our angels for help, we may be surprised by how they answer our prayers, as Patty Patrignelli of Monroe, New York, shares in this story:

Each year my husband and I take our children to an amusement park for a vacation. One year as we walked through the "boardwalk games" area, the children fell in love with one of the prizes: a jumbo rainbow bear. They begged my husband to win it for them, and he tried, losing $20 in the effort.

I'd always told the children to ask their angels for guidance, and that night my son, Tony, asked, "Mom, could the angels help us win that bear?"

"Yes," I assured him. All three children prayed for angelic aid as my husband gallantly tried again. But after losing $40, we admitted defeat and retreated to the hotel.

Seeing my children's disappointment, I told them, "Don't give up on the angels. You never know what they have planned." Little did *I* know that I was about to be more surprised than anyone!

In the parking lot as we approached our car, we saw a teenage boy holding the same bear that the kids had wanted. "How did you win that?" I asked.

"Oh," he said with a smile, "I'm very lucky." Then he turned to the kids, asking, "Would you like to take this bear home?"

"Yes!" they clamored, hugging the stuffed animal with delight. After thanking the boy, we started getting into our car. And suddenly, blowing toward us across the lot, came a roll of three $20 bills, which was exactly what we'd spent trying to win the bear!

Patty reassured her children that prayers are always answered, and the angels proved just how true that is! The bear had colors like a rainbow, an ancient symbol of Divine love—it was a perfect gift from the angels! So was reimbursement of the exact amount they'd spent trying to win the prize. This story is a clear example that all you need to do is ask!

The angels say: "The prayers of children are exquisitely beautiful, as they so clearly ask for what they desire with hearts full of trust and hope."

Faith speeds up the answers
to your prayers. Ask the angels
to buoy yours if it's lagging.

The Grocery Angels

There are all kinds of angels, and not all of them have wings, as Dorothy O. Liles, of Laurel Hill, North Carolina, shares in the following story:

It was 1961, and a time of great discouragement for our family. I was on maternity leave from my job, expecting our fourth child. My husband was sick and out of work.

With unpaid bills and medical expenses mounting, we were becoming anxious. And one particular day when I looked in the kitchen, there was almost nothing left to eat, just a little ground beef and half a box of oatmeal.

"What are we going to do without bread?" my husband asked.

"We'll make it," I said with more conviction than I felt. "I'll mix the oatmeal with the meat to stretch it."

Only after my husband left the room did I allow myself to cry. Wearily, I rolled out the burgers, thinking: *I don't even have any words left to pray.* So I began to whisper the familiar words, "Give us this day our daily bread . . ."

That's when I heard a knock at the door. A woman from my workplace stood there, two bags in her arms. "I hope you won't be offended," she said. "But the strangest thing happened while I was shopping for groceries. Just as I was putting my bread in the cart, I had the idea to buy you a loaf or two. I also took the liberty of buying you a few more items and some candy for the children."

With grateful tears, I accepted her generous gift. A few minutes later, our family joined hands and shared a prayer of gratitude.

But it wasn't long before we started wondering, *But what about tomorrow?*

"Heaven will supply our needs," I reassured my family with renewed faith. "Even if the angels have to call on the President of the United States!"

The very next morning, after the children left for school, a lady came to the door. "I represent the Junior Chamber of Commerce," she explained. "We heard you were going through a rough time, and we'd like to help."

It took several trips to carry all the food she'd brought into the house. Groceries were all over the table, chairs, cabinets, and floor.

There were large bags of flour, rice, sugar, and many other items.

I thanked the woman with tears in my eyes and closed the door. It was only then that I noticed that printed on each bag were the words: *Food Surplus Program, by order of John F. Kennedy, President of the United States!*

My children are grown, and I'm a great-grandmother now, but I've never forgotten that day and the way Heaven sent its earthly angels to supply our daily bread.

Dorothy's story is a beautiful illustration of the way Heaven sometimes inspires everyday people to act as earthly angels. It also shows that when we pray with strong, fervent emotions and a clear idea of what we want, our prayers are answered very quickly. And mothers' prayers for their children seem to receive top priority in Heaven.

Dorothy didn't tell Heaven she needed money for food. She simply asked for food. This allowed Heaven to move quickly, inspiring the earthly angels who delivered what was needed.

The angels say, "When you are tired or worried, you cannot always hear our voices guiding you toward the answer to your prayer. That is why we often speak to you through others. Sometimes we will whisper an answer to a person who then will speak these words directly to you. Other times we will guide a person to help you in a way that lets you know your angels are near.

"Whenever you pray, keep an open mind so that you will notice our answers. Your prayers sprout first as tiny seedlings. As you tend them with faith and guided action, your bumper crop will soon be harvested."

If you get an intuitive feeling to help someone, Heaven is probably enlisting you as an earthly angel at that moment.

A Telephone Call from an Angel

Need a job? Angels run an employment agency that's "out of this world," as Margaret-Ellen Johnson experienced firsthand:

I'd been a homemaker in San Antonio for 15 years when my husband learned that he'd soon be laid off. As a former secretary, I was sure that my skills would still be in demand, and I told my husband, "Don't worry. I'll get a job."

But it wasn't as easy as I'd thought it would be. Although my skills were still up-to-date, no one seemed interested in hiring me, and I was getting concerned. What would we do when my husband's paychecks stopped coming?

Finally, I heard about a really good job. However, even though I could tell that the interview had gone well, the position went to a younger, less-experienced worker. Discouraged, I prayed for help.

A few days later, just before my husband's last day of work, I received a phone call. "This is Betty Smith," the woman on the phone said. "I'm a friend of the manager where you recently interviewed. There's going to be a change with that job soon. If you still want it, call him right away."

"Are you sure?" I hesitated. If they hadn't hired me the first time around, why would they now? But she was so insistent that I made the call.

"Betty who?" the manager asked. Astonished, he added, "I'm the only person who knew that job was reopening!" Still, in spite of the strange way we'd reconnected, he asked me to come back for a second interview—and this time I got the job!

For a while I tried to figure out the identity of my mysterious caller. But no one at the company had ever heard of Betty Smith. So who was she, and how had she known the position was reopening? Now, after 20 years at the perfect job, I can only assume that the wondrous gift was from an angel.

It surely was! Angels often masquerade as helpful strangers. As in Margaret-Ellen's story, they may use the telephone to deliver their message . . . or they may take on human form, coming to Earth just long enough to provide what we need. Most people never realize that they've communicated with a messenger from Heaven until they try to find the stranger later.

The angels say, "Do not hesitate to call upon us when you need help with anything at all. We are with you always—just a prayer, thought, or wish away. It is our greatest pleasure to guide you to the people and situations that bring you peace."

If you're starting a new project, ask the angels to open the door to opportunity and success.

Holiday Dreams Coming True

Although the angels are always with us, somehow they seem closer during the holiday season, as Dianne Byron Schneider of Nassau, New York, shares in the following story:

I grew up in a country town in New York. Even though we weren't wealthy by any means, compared with other families in our area, we did fine. One Christmas, my mom ordered some hats and mittens as a warm gift for some of the poor children in our community. The bill was $30, which was a lot of money at the time, but when the box came with all the hats and mittens, our home was filled with joy.

But then a few days later, a second box arrived containing the exact same items. Mom called the store to tell them that they'd made a mistake. But the clerk couldn't figure out why the second box had been shipped. He just said, "Well, Merry Christmas," and then hung up. My mother was never billed for it.

And ever since, we've been convinced that the angels sent that second box to help Mom make even more children happy that Christmas.

Dianne's mother was acting as an earthly angel that holiday season. So Heaven made the experience even more meaningful by arranging for extra provisions.

The angels love granting children's wishes and prayers, as Veronica LaMere Rivera of Pico Rivera, California, shares:

It was a Monday evening in late October, and my temp assignment was scheduled to finish at the end of the week.

"Mommy, can we go to Kansas this year for Christmas?" my five-year-old son, Martin, asked.

I missed my family in Kansas terribly, but so far I hadn't been able to afford a visit. "I'm not sure," I waffled. "My job ends on Friday and . . ."

Martin looked at me with such regret that my heart ached. But suddenly, his eyes brightened. "Maybe the angels can help," he said, and prayed aloud: "Angels, please help my mom get a job."

The very next morning, my boss approached me, saying, "Your assignment has been extended." I sat there overwhelmed with gratitude, for I knew that Martin's prayer had been heard and answered.

That evening I told my son, "Thanks to your prayer and the angels' answer, we can go to Kansas this Christmas!"

Little Martin demonstrated the pure faith of a child by confidently turning the situation over to Heaven. He instinctively knew that the angels can only help us if we ask.

The angels say, "We await your signal that you would like our intervention, and then we immediately go to work on your behalf. We are not limited as to how we can help you, so allow yourself to be pleasantly surprised by the creative ways in which we answer your prayers."

Ask the angels to assist you with every aspect of the holiday season, including family issues, gift-giving ideas, finances, and your emotional well-being.

ACKNOWLEDGMENTS

From Doreen Virtue: I am so grateful to all of the angels in Heaven and on Earth who are helping all of us along the way. For this particular book, my gratitude extends to the entire *Woman's World* staff, including Stephanie Saible, Naomi Kenan, Amy Oscar, and Dennis Cohen. I am also deeply grateful to everyone at Hay House.

The great folks at *Woman's World* and Hay House are my extended-family members, and I love you all!

From Amy Oscar: My deepest gratitude to Stephanie Saible, *Woman's World*'s editor-in-chief, who was certain our readers would love this miraculous column (which they did); my editors, Naomi Kenan and Andrea Florczak; my spirit sisters, Taryn Phillips-Quinn and Jamie Kiffel; my teacher Caroline Myss, for leading me into my castle; and Doreen Virtue, for showing me what a life lived in light looks like.

Finally, I thank the angels for orchestrating this luscious and remarkable journey.

ABOUT DOREEN VIRTUE

Doreen Virtue, Ph.D., is a doctor of psychology who works with the angelic realm. She is the author of numerous best-selling books and products, including the *Healing with the Angels* book and card deck. She has been featured on *Oprah,* CNN, and *Good Morning America;* and in newspapers and magazines worldwide. Doreen's column, "My Guardian Angel," appears in *Woman's World* magazine weekly.

Doreen teaches classes related to her books and frequently gives audiences angel readings. For information on her products, workshops, and message-board community, or to receive her free monthly e-newsletter, please visit: **www.AngelTherapy.com**.

ABOUT AMY OSCAR

Amy Oscar co-writes and edits the "My Guardian Angel" column for *Woman's World* magazine. She has been gently guiding people along the spiritual path for 25 years. Amy holds certificates in Sacred Contracts and Spiritual Alchemy (from the CMED Institute), and Angel Therapy™. She has studied biography, archetypal patterning, and dream work and is a candidate for a master's/Ph.D. in archetypal psychology.

Amy is the publisher of *As If* magazine. You can contact her for readings or counseling through her Website at: **asifmagazine.com**.

Please send your angel stories by e-mail to: **angels@bauerpublishing.com** or mail them to Angels, *Woman's World* Magazine, 270 Sylvan Avenue, Englewood Cliffs, NJ 07632.

Hay House Titles of Related Interest

THE ANGEL BY MY SIDE: *The True Story of a Dog Who Saved a Man . . . and a Man Who Saved a Dog,* by Mike Lingenfelter and David Frei

ANIMALS AND THE AFTERLIFE: *True Stories of Our Best Friends' Journey Beyond Death,* by Kim Sheridan

THE LAW OF ATTRACTION: *The Basics of the Teachings of Abraham™,* by Esther and Jerry Hicks

MIRACLES, by Stuart Wilde

THE GAME OF LIFE *(Hay House Classics)*, by Florence Scovel Shinn

YOUR IMMORTAL REALITY: *How to Break the Cycle of Birth and Death*, by Gary Renard

THE TIMES OF OUR LIVES: *Extraordinary True Stories of Synchronicity, Destiny, Meaning, and Purpose,* by Louise L. Hay & Friends

All of the above are available at your local bookstore, or may be ordered by contacting Hay House.

We hope you enjoyed this Hay House book. If you'd like to receive a free catalog featuring additional Hay House books and products, or if you'd like information about the Hay Foundation, please contact:

Hay House, Inc.
P.O. Box 5100
Carlsbad, CA 92018-5100

(760) 431-7695 or **(800) 654-5126**
(760) 431-6948 (fax) or **(800) 650-5115 (fax)**
www.hayhouse.com® • www.hayfoundation.org

Published and distributed in Australia by: Hay House Australia Pty. Ltd., 18/36 Ralph St., Alexandria NSW 2015 • *Phone:* 612-9669-4299 *Fax:* 612-9669-4144 • www.hayhouse.com.au

Published and distributed in the United Kingdom by: Hay House UK, Ltd., 292B Kensal Rd., London W10 5BE • *Phone:* 44-20-8962-1230 *Fax:* 44-20-8962-1239 • www.hayhouse.co.uk

Published and distributed in the Republic of South Africa by: Hay House SA (Pty), Ltd., P.O. Box 990, Witkoppen 2068 *Phone/Fax:* 27-11-467-8904 • orders@psdprom.co.za www.hayhouse.co.za

Published in India by: Hay House Publishers India, Muskaan Complex, Plot No. 3, B-2, Vasant Kunj, New Delhi 110 070 • *Phone:* 91-11-4176-1620 *Fax:* 91-11-4176-1630 • www.hayhouse.co.in

Distributed in Canada by: Raincoast, 9050 Shaughnessy St., Vancouver, B.C. V6P 6E5 • *Phone:* (604) 323-7100 *Fax:* (604) 323-2600 • www.raincoast.com

Tune in to **HayHouseRadio.com®** for the best in inspirational talk radio featuring top Hay House authors! And, sign up via the Hay House USA Website to receive the Hay House online newsletter and stay informed about what's going on with your favorite authors. You'll receive bimonthly announcements about Discounts and Offers, Special Events, Product Highlights, Free Excerpts, Giveaways, and more!
www.hayhouse.com®